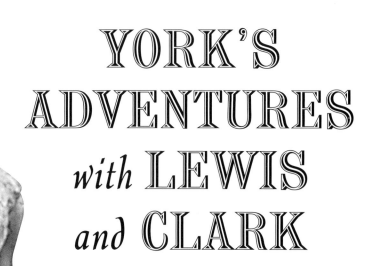

YORK'S ADVENTURES
with LEWIS
and CLARK

◆

*An African-American's
Part in the
Great Expedition*

◆

By
Rhoda
Blumberg

◌ Collins
An Imprint of HarperCollinsPublishers

For Jerry, of course!

ALSO BY RHODA BLUMBERG

Commodore Perry in the Land of the Shogun

Full Steam Ahead: The Race to Build a Transcontinental Railroad

The Great American Gold Rush

The Incredible Journey of Lewis and Clark

The Remarkable Voyages of Captain Cook

Shipwrecked!: The True Adventures of a Japanese Boy

What's the Deal?: Jefferson, Napoleon, and the Louisiana Purchase

The African-American sculptor Ed Hamilton was asked to memorialize York for the Lewis and Clark bicentennial. After "trying to see the world through [York's] eyes so that [he could] create his face," Hamilton began sketching and planning the bronze statue that now overlooks the Ohio River in Louisville, Kentucky. The jacket front features a detail of the sculpture against the backdrop of the Bitterroot Mountains. The statue is shown in full on the title page.

James J. Holmberg, editor of Dear Brother: Letters of William Clark to Jonathan Clark, *lectures frequently about York. He is the curator of special collections at the Filson Historical Society in Louisville, Kentucky.*

Collins is an imprint of HarperCollins Publishers.

Library of Congress Cataloging-in-Publication Data
Blumberg, Rhoda.
York's adventures with Lewis and Clark : an African-American's part in the great expedition / by Rhoda Blumberg. — 1st ed.   p.   cm.
   Summary: Relates the adventures of York, a slave and "body servant" to William Clark, who journeyed west with the Lewis and Clark Expedition of 1804–1806. Includes bibliographical references.
   ISBN-10: 0-06-009111-8 (trade bdg.) — ISBN-13: 978-0-06-009111-8 (trade bdg.)
   ISBN-10: 0-06-009112-6 (lib. bdg.) — ISBN-13: 978-0-06-009112-5 (lib. bdg.)
   ISBN-10: 0-06-009113-4 (pbk.) — ISBN-13: 978-0-06-009113-2 (pbk.)
   1. York, ca. 1775–ca. 1815—Juvenile literature. 2. Lewis and Clark Expedition (1804–1806)—Juvenile literature. 3. Slaves—West (U.S.)—Biography—Juvenile literature. 4. West (U.S.)—Biography—Juvenile literature. [1. York, ca. 1775–ca. 1815. 2. Lewis and Clark Expedition (1804–1806). 3. Slaves. 4. African Americans—Biography. 5. West (U.S.)—Biography.] I. Title.
F592.7.Y67B57 2004   971.804'2—dc21   2003009425

Typography by Carla Weise
❖

Contents

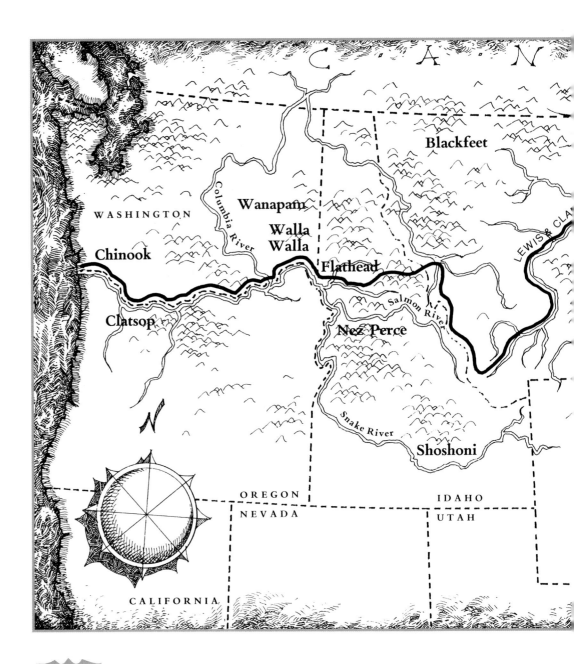

York traveled through this territory. The states shown on the map did not exist at the time of the expedition, and the location of the Indian tribes is approximate.

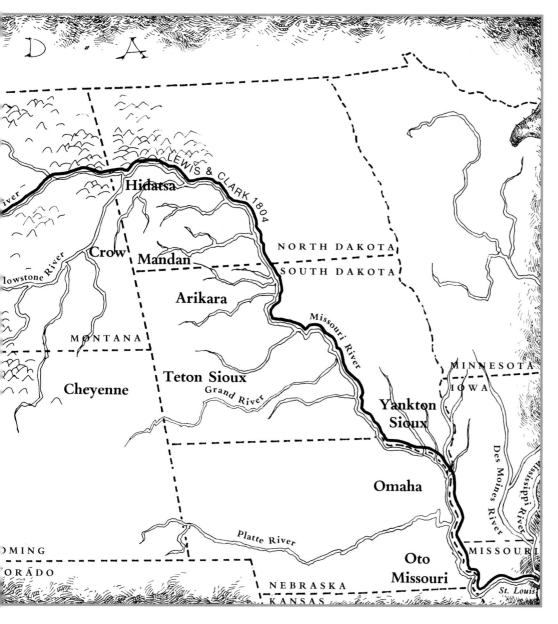

Introduction

By James J. Holmberg

The overwhelming majority of slaves in the America of the late eighteenth and early nineteenth centuries lived lives that are lost to history. Even their slave names are not often known. York has not suffered that fate. But there are still gaps—and you may find them interesting to think about as you read about his life.

My interest in York began when I was a child traveling the Lewis and Clark trail on family vacations and saw references to him. But the facts were few. It wasn't until the publication in 1985 of Robert Betts's *In Search of York* that a comprehensive and well-balanced study was available. However, much was still unknown, especially about his post-expedition life. Then, in 1988, a collection of William Clark's letters to his brother Jonathan was discovered in an attic in Louisville, Kentucky.

I edited the letters, in *Dear Brother: Letters of William Clark to Jonathan Clark*, so that people could read, in William Clark's own words, what happened to York after the expedition. The original letters are now in the collection of the Filson Historical Society.

Other documents, many of them also at the Filson, trace York's life to November 1815. He was still a slave, estranged from his master and apparently separated from a wife whom he loved very much. A seventeen-year gap exists before we know more about York. In 1832 William Clark told the famous American author Washington Irving that he had freed York and set him up in a freight-hauling business. Clark also said that York lost the business, regretted getting his freedom, and died in Tennessee while returning to him. Is this true?

Are there documents out there that will fill in the gaps? Will we learn the name of York's wife? Will we know if they had children? Will documents emerge to prove or disprove what Clark told Irving? Can greater interest in the history of African-Americans lead to more discoveries? I continue to search, as do others.

Fortunately recognition of York is growing today. As the bicentennial commemoration of the Lewis and Clark expedition unfolds, appreciation for what he accomplished and for what he symbolizes is increasing. In January 2001, President Bill Clinton made York an honorary sergeant in the United States Army. In April 2001, York was inducted into the Hall of Great Westerners at the National Cowboy and Western Heritage Museum. York was individually honored at Thomas Jefferson's home, Monticello, in January 2003 during opening ceremonies of the Lewis and Clark Bicentennial. A heroic-sized bronze statue, created by nationally acclaimed sculptor Ed Hamilton, looks out on the Ohio River and westward from the Louisville waterfront—a fitting honor to York by the city that he called home for most of his life. Actors portray York in first-person performances across the nation. A documentary film about him is in production. Books, articles, and poetry are being written about him. And this is not all.

As you read *York's Adventures with Lewis and Clark*, think about York's place in history. History lets us look back and, in looking back, we have an opportunity to learn from the past. It's only now that we are beginning to truly acknowledge and celebrate the contributions this enslaved man made to our country.

1. THE EARLY YEARS

Imagine a boy of twelve or thirteen being the slave of a fourteen-year-old master! That took place on a plantation in Caroline County, Virginia, in 1784, when an enslaved black boy was assigned to be Master William Clark's personal "body servant." Like many other slaves, this boy didn't have the legal right to a last name. Family names were for whites only. He was just York, called "that Negro York" or "that boy York."[1]

York and William had been playmates ever since they were old enough to walk. Growing up, they played together as equals, roamed in nearby woods, and taught themselves to swim in its streams and ponds. These carefree days were fated to end. As soon as York and William became adults—both over the age of twelve—they were bound together in a changed relationship. The contrast was as clear as white against black. William became the master whose commands had to be obeyed; York was his slave, his lackey, who had to heed all of William's wishes.

One could say that York was lucky that John Clark, his owner, chose him to become body servant for William, the youngest of his six sons. It was, indeed, a privileged position. York had been singled out not only because he was William's companion, but also because he was strong enough to be a bodyguard, efficient enough to accompany an up-and-coming Virginia gentleman, and smart enough to use good judgment.

All that is known about York's parents are their names, which were listed in John Clark's will, dated 1799. York's father was called Old York; his mother was named Rose. Old York may have been John Clark's personal servant, and Rose may have been a house servant.

A household slave

Black household servants, like York, were "upper-class slaves." As a personal body servant, York slept in the Clarks' home within earshot of William. He wore clothing that matched the style and quality of his master's (probably hand-me-downs from William and his older brothers). He ate fine foods from the Clark family kitchen, acquired polished manners, and had a way of speaking that sounded "white," with hardly a trace of a slave's speech patterns.

He was much better off than Clark's field-workers. After turning twelve, these slaves were ordered to work from dawn to dark tending the plantation's tobacco crops and vegetable fields. They wore coarse shirts and trousers that were made by slave women. Their masters supplied shoes, to be used when the weather was raw or when the ground was rugged. Most of the time they went barefoot. Their diet featured corn, molasses, beans, and gristly scraps of pork. To sleep, they coiled themselves on top of straw-covered boards inside dingy huts where floors were dirt and tables and chairs were boxes.

All slaves—even household servants like York—were forbidden to learn reading and writing. Books were deemed dangerous in the hands of slaves, because reading about freedom might incite them to revolt against their bondage. They might start a rebellion. They might run away. It was a crime to teach them to read, give them books, or show them how to write.

Masters were constantly haunted by the threat of slave revolts. They were so alarmed that slaves who *tried* learning to read were whipped, branded, or had their ears cropped; sometimes they were

A runaway slave

put to death.[2] Owners were so edgy that horns and drums were banned because slaves sounding them could signal the start of a rebellion. That had happened in 1739, when slaves near Charleston, South Carolina, used drums to send messages to one another, then rose up in pitched battle against their masters. Before this uprising was put down, thirty white men and forty-four black men had been killed. Stories about this revolt, called the Stono Uprising, were passed down by the enslaved and the planters for generations.

Many southerners were also upset by the existence of free blacks. They feared that the very sight of them set a bad example for slaves, who

might be prompted to seek their own liberty. Free blacks had to carry certificates of freedom in every southern state at all times, but even with these identification papers, they risked being seized and sold into slavery. In the South, special patrols were set up to cross-examine free blacks and arrest stray slaves.

If York wished to wander outside of the plantation, he had to carry a handwritten pass from his owner, called a "remit," for his own protection. Any white person could stop him, and if he did not have this pass he could be whipped before being returned to his master. Fear of straying slaves was so strong that, according to codes in South Carolina and Georgia, it was legal to kill any slave who was found away from his or her plantation if he or she was unaccompanied by a white person. Runaway slaves posed a serious problem that worried owners. The problem became especially alarming during the Revolutionary War, when an estimated thirty thousand slaves ran away from Virginia and a total of one hundred thousand escaped from the South to find freedom for themselves.[3]

News about freed slaves and runaway slaves undoubtedly reached slave quarters, as did worrisome reports about William's five older

Slaves who didn't carry a pass outside the plantation could be beaten, arrested, or killed.

brothers, who were fighting for American freedom. York was four or five, and William was only six years old, when they learned that William's brother John was imprisoned on a British ship. Everyone on the plantation was affected by the news. John came home after six years of prison, his health broken, and he died in 1783. Richard died during the war; his body was never found. Jonathan, Edmund, and George Rogers survived the war and returned as heroes. George Rogers Clark was famous. He had led astounding battles that defeated British forces in the Ohio Valley.[4]

The Clark brothers' homecomings must have been a source of pride and elation for family, house servants, and field hands. How fascinating it must have been for York and William to hear firsthand accounts of war battles and conquests—examples of endurance, bravery, and daring that they hoped to emulate when they grew up.

Ten Dollars Reward.

RANAWAY on the twelfth day of April laſt, GABRIEL, a ſlave the property of Mrs Mary Bolling, of Peterſburg; obtained leave of abſence for 15 days to go to Mr. Benjamin Marable's in Glouceſter County—and the ſaid ſlave not having returned yet, and there being good reaſon to believe that he is ſtill lurking in that neighbourhood—the above ſum will be paid for having him confined in jail ſo that his owner gets him again, or a reward of Twenty Dollars, excluſive of what the law allows if brought home. Gabriel is a black man, about 30 years old, long viſage, about 6 feet high, fond of drink, and by trade a weaver. He was purchaſed from the eſtate of the late Colonel Peyton, and is well known in that part of the country. All perſons are forewarned from harbouring, employing or carrying the ſaid fellow out of the State.

Richeson Booker.

Peterſburg, October 30, 1800. eotf

However, to be realistic, York could not look forward to a brilliant future. He had to learn lessons harder to understand than anything in books. As a young boy he had to be drilled to endure humiliation and to acknowledge all white people as masters who had overwhelming power over him. Plantation slaves taught him to accept his fate as an underling: As a slave he owned nothing, not even the clothes on his back. Looked upon as property, he could be bought and sold at his owner's will. York knew that blacks who did not obey could be beaten until their backs were bloody. It must have been dismaying and degrading to be told that he was doomed to be a slave for his entire lifetime, and that slavery was hereditary. It would be handed

5

*Black children
could be sold
and taken from
their parents.*

down to his children, and in turn to their offspring. The miserable, hopeless condition was presumably fated to endure forever.

Even though the Clarks were kind people who treated their slaves well, York had to realize that if crops failed or his owner became strapped for cash, he might be sold for needed money. His family must have warned him that if he did not please his owner, he could be sold, shipped, and delivered to another owner who lived faraway. There might be a direct sale to another master, or he could be placed on an auction block, where every part of his body would be inspected and where bidders known to be brutal could buy him.

The threat of separation loomed large. New owners might live so far away that York would never see his family again. In the eyes of the law, marriage between slaves had no legal force. A master reserved the right to separate mother and father and sell them to different buyers. There was always talk about slaves whose children, parents, husbands, and wives were sold and sent away for life.

York had to realize that his fate was completely controlled by his master.

Moving West

In 1784, about the year that York was made William's personal slave, the Clarks gave up their plantation in Virginia and moved west, to the rough frontier country of Kentucky. The move was made because, like other plantation owners, John Clark did not know about rotating crops to enrich the soil. Therefore he had to find new land for cultivating his main crop, tobacco. He hoped to enjoy prosperity in a backcountry where soil was said to be fertile and where wilderness was known to be rich with game.

The move began in October, when York and about twenty other slaves traveled overland with the Clark family to the town of Pittsburgh, the outfitting point for pioneers. They were forced to remain there during the winter, icebound until the frozen Ohio River thawed in the spring of 1785. Like a thousand other families also heading out from Pittsburgh that year, the Clarks loaded their household goods, livestock, and slaves on flatboats, then rode down the river to Kentucky.

Clearing and planting fields, building a two-story main house, a separate kitchen house, a gristmill, and setting up slave cabins meant hard labor for all slaves, including York. One of the Clark men was probably nearby, giving orders and supervising construction. The new plantation was named Mulberry Hill.[1]

Indians were, understandably, up in arms against settlers who were claiming their hunting grounds in Kentucky. They attacked, scalped, and killed pioneers and set farms on fire. The pioneers in turn attacked, scalped, and killed Indians. Although slaves were forbidden to use firearms and he was only thirteen or fourteen years old, York was given a gun to hunt game and help protect the Clark property against Indian raids. John Clark had probably received a permit from the justice of the peace that allowed a slave to own a gun. There may have been Indian raids against Mulberry Hill, but these were not recorded.

William Clark remarked that he was "always accompanied by his little Negro boy, York."[2] It was customary for a southern gentleman to be with his body servant. Together they rode horseback—unusual, for as a rule slaves were not permitted to use horses, lest they gallop away to escape. York often traveled with his master to Louisville, Kentucky, an important river town that was only four miles from the plantation. Louisville was a gateway to downriver trade. William arranged to have tobacco, whiskey, and other plantation products sent to New Orleans by way of the Ohio and Mississippi Rivers. From New Orleans these were shipped to ports on the east coast of the United States and to England, where tobacco was in great demand.

At Louisville a slave auction block and the courthouse next to it must have been chilling for York. He must have known that a man's estimated sale value in the slave market was approximately five hundred dollars—about four times more than a black female's estimated worth.[3] He probably knew that no black person was allowed to testify in any southern court of law—not even if he witnessed a murder! Blacks could be sentenced to die for trivial wrongdoings. York undoubtedly heard about a slave named Tom who had been condemned to death in that very court just because he had stolen "two and three-fourths yards of cambric [cotton cloth] and some ribbon and thread."[4] The auction block and the courthouse were horrifying reminders of grim truths about slavery.

Between 1789 and 1796, York's whereabouts remain a mystery. There are no records. York did not know how to write, and Clark mentioned York in just one letter to a sister. It stated that "my Boy" [York] visited his army camp in 1795, probably to drop off supplies for his master.[5] We do know from family letters that in 1789, at the age of nineteen, Clark left home to fight Indians with the Kentucky militia. Three years later he enlisted in the army and became a lieutenant. Army officers were allowed to bring along "personal servants" to serve them and accompany them on the battlefield. But there is no mention that York was with Clark. York may have spent those years as one of the plantation's house slaves. In 1796, after being away over four years, with only periodic visits to his family, Clark resigned from the army and returned home.

When William Clark's father, John Clark, died in 1799, York, then twenty-seven or twenty-eight years old, legally became William's property. According to John Clark's will, William inherited the family plantation of Mulberry Hill, all its equipment, livestock, thousands of acres of land in Kentucky, a still, and eight slaves, including "one Negroe man named York," York's mother, Rose, and his father "Old York and their two children [Nancy and Juba]."[6] Nancy and Juba were York's sister and brother, but this is all we know about them. Slaves were also left to John's other sons and to sons-in-law—not to his daughters, for at that time, husbands owned and controlled all property. (Bequeathing slaves was traditional. William's father was only eight years old when he inherited Old York and other slaves from *his* father.)

From 1800 to 1802, because of "frequent [business] reasons

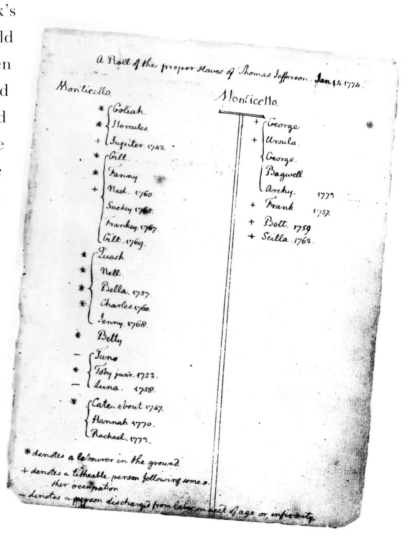

to Visit the Eastern States & Washington," York accompanied Clark on visits to President Jefferson. York and Clark had been acquainted with Jefferson when they were children in Virginia, for Jefferson's home was just a short distance away from the Clark plantation. And Clark had become a friend of the president's secretary, Meriwether Lewis, when they had both served in the army. They enjoyed each other's company even when Clark became Lewis's commanding officer.

President Thomas Jefferson wanted Lewis to prepare an expedition across the continent. The president wanted western lands to be claimed as United States territory in order to keep England, France, and Spain from hemming in the United States.

According to Jefferson's vision, a trip to the Pacific Ocean could be accomplished by river. Like many scientists of his time, he envisioned a transcontinental waterway that stretched from the Missouri River to the Pacific Ocean. In addition to exploring the land, finding sources for furs, and making maps, the explorers were to befriend

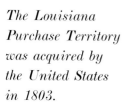

The Louisiana Purchase Territory was acquired by the United States in 1803.

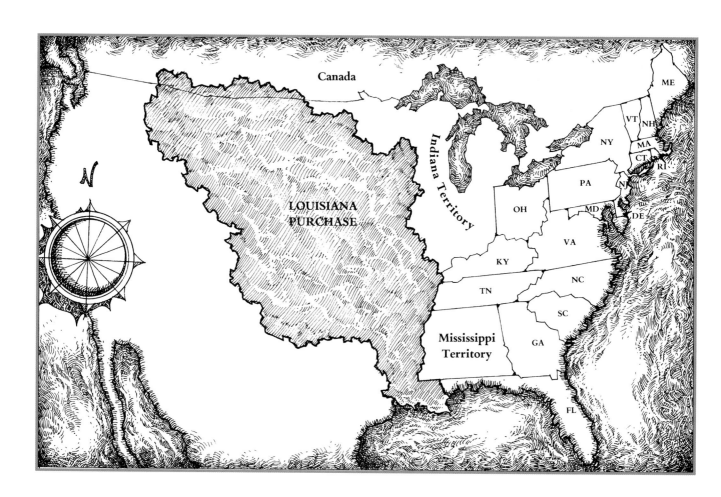

Indian tribes; study their customs, beliefs, and languages; and write detailed descriptions about the animals, plants, and minerals they found as they traveled across the country. Lewis was directed to describe everything from soil to stars.

It was Lewis who determined to have his friend William Clark accompany him. And it was Clark who was intent upon bringing his manservant with him. York was destined to experience events that would profoundly change the course of his life.

One Black Man

YORK WAS PROBABLY thirty-one or thirty-two and Clark thirty-three years old when, in 1803, Clark finally received a letter from Meriwether Lewis inviting him to become co-captain of an extraordinary expedition that would cross North America. "If therefore there is anything . . . which would induce you to participate with me in its fatigues, its dangers and its honors," Lewis wrote, "believe me there is no man on earth with whom I should feel equal pleasure in sharing them as with yourself."[1] Clark was so excited, he replied with a letter the very next day. "My friend," he wrote, "I do assure you that no man lives whith whome I would perfur to undertake Such a Trip &c. as yourself, and I shall arrange my matters as well as I can against your arrival here."[2]

Some time before 1803, York had fallen in love with a neighbor's slave. He had to have William Clark's permission to visit her, and he also needed his master's consent to marry her. It would have been so much more convenient to Clark had York married a field hand or house servant who lived on the family plantation, because children of a slave marriage stayed with the wife and belonged to the wife's owner. That would have meant babies—new slaves—for Mulberry

Meriwether Lewis

William Clark

Hill. In this case the neighbor was to receive the "benefits"—offspring—of the marriage. Perhaps there was no slave girl on the plantation who suited York, or it may have been that Clark wished to please his servant. Another master might have bought a black girl for York so that the couple could remain on his property. Instead Clark agreed to the match—or perhaps he arranged it with his neighbor. We do not know. In fact, we do not even know the name of the woman York married, the date of the wedding, or whether they had children. But as subsequent events will show, York loved her very much.

There was no minister or priest to perform the ceremony, for a slave marriage was not a religious ritual. Instead the master might hastily tell the couple, "You are married." White friends of the owner and plantation slaves were often invited to the "Big House" to witness the occasion and enjoy refreshments. The ceremony did *not* contain the traditional pledge "'Til death do us part," for there was never any assurance that the couple would always be together. There was no marriage contract, no "lawful wedlock." The marriage could be destroyed at any time by the sale of one or both partners by their owners. The couple could also be separated forever should one of the owners move far away, taking their enslaved people with him.

To enliven the occasion, after Clark told them they were married, York and his bride probably jumped over a broomstick. This was an African wedding ritual signifying their leap into a new life; they were sweeping away the old with a broom and welcoming a new beginning with a jump. It was traditional to serve a sumptuous meal of meats and sweets—special treats that plantation slaves savored only when invited to a wedding conducted by white people. York and his bride may have continued to celebrate in the slave quarters by dancing to the rhythms of singing and hand clapping. (Slaves were not allowed to own or use musical instruments lest they sound alerts of rebellion.) Then York was probably permitted to stay with his bride at her home for a few days before returning to Clark.

York was to be far from his wife for close to three years while he accompanied his master on a daring, dangerous expedition. Lewis had asked Clark to find "some good hunters, stout, healthy, unmarried young men, accustomed to the woods, and capable of bearing bodily fatigue to a pretty considerable degree."[3] Although married, York unquestionably qualified for the expedition. This tall, big, muscular black man was an able hunter, a strong swimmer, and a sturdy hiker. He was also an intelligent companion and a dedicated servant, ever ready to follow orders and care for his master's needs. York would be ideal for any expedition. He would be separated from his wife, but as an enslaved man, he had no choice but to follow his master.

York

Clark had a hard time finding others with qualifications comparable to York's. When he asked around for volunteers, many young men jumped at the chance to join the expedition because they sought adventure and wanted the large land grant that the government promised to each recruit. Clark chose carefully, recruiting seven of the "best woodsmen and hunters" in the Louisville area. He deliberately rejected "Gentlemen's sons" because they were not accustomed to obeying orders, experiencing hardships, and enduring hard labor.[4] Even though he and Lewis were southern gentlemen, both of them felt that most other men in their aristocratic class had lived sheltered lives and would not be able to face the rigors and dangers of wilderness exploration.

The men Clark chose were on trial, subject to the approval of Lewis. The two men Lewis brought with him were approved by

Clark. Most of the expedition's "Corps of Discovery" were recruited from army posts in Tennessee, Illinois, Kentucky, and Missouri. Lewis and Clark believed they had found soldiers "whose characters for sobriety, integrity and other necessary qualifications make them suitable."[5] The abilities to read, write, and swim were not "necessary qualifications." Some of the men were illiterate, and quite a few couldn't swim.

All recruits received monthly salaries: five dollars for soldiers, eight dollars for sergeants, and twenty-five dollars for interpreters. York was in a different category. He was a slave and, as a rule, slaves *never* received salaries. York was the only man on the Lewis and Clark expedition who was not on the payroll. He would not receive a cent for his labor.

According to President Thomas Jefferson, an exploratory trip to the Pacific Ocean was important for the nation.

2. HEADING WEST

Lewis and his party sailed down the Ohio and joined forces with Clark at Louisville. Lewis hired a temporary crew to handle a keelboat and red pirogue (an open boat made from a log), and he brought along some men. Clark, York, and seven more recruits met Lewis's group at the falls of the Ohio at Louisville. These nine recruits were known as the "nine young men from Kentucky."[1]

Lewis, like Clark, was a slaveholder. However, he didn't bring along a body servant, perhaps because none of his slaves had the strength and daring needed for dangerous challenges. A pet Newfoundland dog named Seaman accompanied Lewis. He had purchased the dog while in Pittsburgh buying supplies for the expedition.

Clark joined Lewis with "hand and Heart."[2] Time had not weakened their unusually firm friendship. Lewis had promised Clark that both of them would share leadership as co-captains of the expedition. However the War Department refused to rank Clark as a captain, officially listing him as a second lieutenant. This decision dismayed Lewis. Determined that no man on the expedition would ever know about Clark's lower rank, he decided that Clark would be called "captain" anyway.

The expedition left the falls of the Ohio on October 26, 1803. The all-important foundation of the Corps of Discovery had been laid. The group continued down the Ohio River, picking up more recruits on the way. They also hired an interpreter, George Drouillard, who was skilled at sign language, scouting, and hunting. He was the son of a Shawnee mother and a French-Canadian father.

Riding the Ohio was rough. One of the boats leaked, and in places the river was so shallow the boat's hull scraped bottom so it couldn't sail or be rowed. Oxen and horses had to be hired to pull it into deeper water. When the boats reached the Mississippi, the men found it a treacherous, turbulent river with uprooted trees riding its waters.

In December the captains halted the expedition and set up winter quarters, which they called Camp Wood (also Camp Dubois). It was near the Mississippi River, opposite the mouth of the Missouri River. Clark wrote that the location was "as comfortable as could be expected," and he described the scenery as "butifull beyond discription."[3]

At the start many of the men undoubtedly wondered how York would fit in. In line with the prejudices of the time, they believed that black people were inferior human beings who had little feeling and low intelligence. On an expedition that was expected to take at least two years, some undoubtedly asked themselves how they could tolerate having a slave in their group. York was surely troubled too. Because he was a slave, he must have feared he would be disdained and singled out to do demeaning, disagreeable tasks for everyone.

At Camp Wood York worked side by side with white men, possibly for the first time in his life. They set up tents, cleared land, cut logs, and built huts that would protect them from winter weather.

"Captain Clark & his men building a line of Huts," an 1810 engraving

York used the skills he had acquired when he helped construct a house and huts at Mulberry Hill. His intelligence, stamina, and strength were undoubtedly impressive.

The camp was eighteen easy miles from St. Louis, which was then a settlement with about a thousand inhabitants. Fur traders and trappers had used St. Louis as their headquarters ever since it was founded as a trading post in 1764. It was a place where beaver skins were accepted as money. Although the men under Lewis and Clark were not allowed to leave camp, York, as Clark's servant, went to town occasionally. He stayed with Clark at the home of Auguste Chouteau, a wealthy fur trader. Chouteau gave Clark journals and maps of the Missouri and located experienced river pilots whom Clark hired for the expedition.

Clark trained and disciplined the Corps of Discovery while Lewis gathered additional information for their journey and bought additional provisions in St. Louis. As a servant who was accustomed to commands and as an experienced hunter who was skilled with guns, York usually accompanied Clark.

York probably helped pack the following goods into barrels, bales, and boxes:

- twenty-one bales of gifts for Indians (including fishhooks, mirrors, earrings, combs, scissors, red paint, blue beads, feathered hats, ribbons, leggings, brass kettles, and corn grinders)
- seven bales of "necessary store" (including blankets, clothing, rifles, a medicine chest, and a writing desk)
- food (including fifty kegs of pork, thirty barrels of flour, and six hundred pounds of grease)
- instruments (including a telescope, magnet, quadrant, sextant, chronometer, and compasses)
- books (an almanac and books about history, explorations, botany, mineralogy, and astronomy)

A total of twenty-three thousand pounds of goods! It had to be lugged and loaded onto the boats—heavy cargo to be rowed and towed up rivers.

The Lewis and Clark expedition spent five months at Camp Wood. Clark drilled the recruits in military fashion so that all would be better able to face unknown dangers.[4]

Was York pleased to be told that his name was included as a member of the expedition? On the list of the men leaving Camp Wood, Clark included "2 of us [Lewis and Clark] and York."[5] His role as body servant was no longer a perpetual task. He was not looked down upon by everybody, and was increasingly treated as almost equal.

Many American Indians the Corps were to encounter considered York superior to his white companions.

Whippings and Powwows

MAY 14, 1804: Clark, York, and the recruits left their winter quarters at Camp Wood, "hoisted Sails and Set out [on the Missouri River] in high spirits for the western Expedition."[1] Their boats kept banging against floating logs and scraping against sunken lumber until, after two days, they docked at the village of St. Charles. They spent five days there waiting for Lewis, who had been delayed in St. Louis buying additional equipment for the voyage. At St. Charles the men bought more supplies and rearranged their tons of cargo. One evening they attended a dance the townspeople held. It was fun—too much fun for three of the men, who stayed out all night without permission. A jury made up of five of the men sentenced them to be flogged.

York witnessed the whippings, which were staged to pain and shame the guilty ones in front of the entire Corps. Perhaps until that time York presumed that cruel floggings were used just—and unjustly—for disobedient slaves and for white criminals. He may not have realized that whippings were common practice in armies, navies, and even on commercial ships.

The day after Lewis arrived, the Corps sailed away from St. Charles. Racing currents and sudden shallows kept the boats from making headway. In many places some of the men jumped into the river to push their boats off sandbars and steer them away from floating branches. Because he could swim, York was probably of great value in the water, shoving, guiding, and freeing the boats.

There were also days of smooth sailing, carefree travel, and fine camping. Clark could often be seen strolling along the riverbank, carrying an umbrella, which he used as a sunshade, not as a rain shield—

hardly the usual picture of a tough frontiersman. He was also clean shaven. Even when roughing it in the wilderness, no beards were allowed (with exceptions made for interpreters and boatmen, who had not been recruited into the army).

Because mosquitoes pestered everyone, a remedy was found. The captains bought three hundred pounds of buffalo grease from a fur trapper whose barge was riding the river. The men slathered this grease on their skins to prevent more bites. They also used it for cooking.

Lewis and Clark kept journals, made maps, charted weather, analyzed soil, measured grasses, studied stars, and sketched wildlife. They would eventually supply President Jefferson with detailed reports about the languages, habits, and customs of Indian tribes. Writing about his slave was not a priority for Clark, but he did mention York in his journal and in letters from time to time.

One week after leaving St. Charles, Clark wrote that his "Servant York Swam to the Sand bar to geather Greens for Dinner, and returned with a Sufficient quantity of wild [watercress] or Tung grass."[2] It made a tasty salad, and a great vegetable side dish when boiled. Once again, York used the swimming skills he had acquired during his childhood, when he and Clark played together in streams and ponds.

York hunted game. He and

Sketch of a sage grouse, from William Clark's journal

five recruits who were also expert hunters supplied meat for enormous appetites. According to Captain Lewis, "[I]t requires 4 deer, an Elk and a deer, or one buffaloe, to supply us plentuflly for 24 hours."[3] That's a hefty amount to use up in one day! Menus changed as the types of wildlife changed. Venison, beaver, and buffalo were delicious dishes, as were grapes gathered from vines, cherries from trees, and berries from bushes. There was also an incredible variety of river fish. Clark sometimes measured and classified the fish before having them cooked.

Well fed, and usually in good health, at times men sickened from sunstroke, stomachaches, and fevers. It is miraculous that only one man lost his life during the entire expedition. He was Sergeant Charles Floyd, who died three months after the expedition started. He may have had appendicitis, a condition without cure at that time. The Corps did not have a doctor in its ranks. Lewis had invited a physician from Virginia to join the expedition, "provided he could get

In some places there were buffalo as far as the eye could see.

ready by three the next morning," but the doctor couldn't leave that quickly, so Lewis left without him.[4] The Corps depended upon medicines that a Philadelphia physician had given to Lewis. During Floyd's illness, when no remedies could cure his stomach pains, it was York who took care of him until he died. The men buried Floyd "with the honors of war, much lamented."[5]

Summer brought searing heat, sudden storms, unruliness—and the occasional need for strict discipline. York and the rest of the Corps watched floggings.

- In June Private Hugh Hall received fifty lashes on his bare back for stealing whiskey, and Private John Collins one hundred lashes for being drunk on post and permitting the theft.
- In July Private Alexander Hamilton Willard was convicted of sleeping at his post while doing sentry duty. According to regulations, he could have received a death sentence. Instead he endured one hundred lashes on his bare back, each day for four days, at sunset.
- August Moses Reed was court-martialed for deserting and stealing a rifle. He was sentenced to run the gauntlet (between two rows of men) four times, "that each man with nine switches should punish him."[6] That amounted to about five hundred lashes. In Reed's case, three chiefs of the Oto tribe were upset when they heard that a beating would take place. They were shocked to learn that this was a custom of our country, but after Lewis and Clark explained the need for this kind of discipline, they agreed that the punishment was just, and they, too, watched the whipping.
- The last flogging took place in October 1804. At that time an Arikara chief who was with the explorers was so appalled that he shed tears and cried aloud that his people never whipped anyone, not even children.

The Corps also assembled to watch powwows. The expedition's first Indian powwow occurred on August 3, 1804, at a place Clark named Council Bluff (in present-day Nebraska). A small group of a dozen Oto and Missouri Indians visited the camp. York joined the rest of the Corps under the shade of the keelboat's main sail, which had been set up as an awning. Captain Lewis addressed the Indians as "children" and told them that "the great chief of the Seventeen great nations [the seventeen states]" was "their only father . . . their only friend." After warning his "red children" to "avoid the council of bad birds [the English and French Canadians]," he promised that American traders would give them better goods on better terms than they ever received before.[7] A French-Canadian trader who lived with these Indians acted as interpreter. Lewis hung medals around the necks of the natives and gave them gifts of flags, mirrors, garters, gunpowder, face paint, leggings, blankets, and whiskey. As a grand finale, to impress them with Americans' military might, the soldiers of the Corps paraded carrying rifles, and Lewis shot off a gun.

An Omaha chief wearing a peace medal

York was to hear the same speech and watch gift-giving ceremonies and parades before the Omaha and many other tribes. Although the Americans repeated this routine with a certain sameness, each performance was a new, entrancing show. Indian tribes differed so much in attitudes, costumes, and customs that watching them was spellbinding. Powwows took everyone away from routine drills and tiresome tasks.

The First Winter

IN LATE AUGUST the expedition reached Sioux territory (near present-day Yankton, South Dakota). The Sioux were reputedly quick to kill strangers. Most white traders were so afraid they didn't dare do business with them. Even so, the captains dispatched two of their men to a Yankton Sioux village to invite the Indians to a powwow. Much to their relief, they received a friendly welcome. Five chiefs and seventy warriors came back with them "very much decorated with paint, porcupine quills and feathers, large leggings and moccasins—all with buffalo robes of different colors."[1] Some of them wore necklaces of bear claws.

York heard Lewis give his usual speech about the Great Father in Washington who wanted to take care of his "red children." He undoubtedly realized that, like "black" people, "red" ones were considered inferior by "whites."

When the meeting was over, York watched Indian boys hold an archery contest. The explorers gave beads as prizes to the winners. At night he saw the Yanktons dance around the campfire to the rhythm of songs, rattles, and drums. Lewis and Clark awarded the performers tobacco, bells, and knives. The next day, after hearing that the Yanktons would send a delegation to the president in Washington, Lewis and Clark handed the Indians more trinkets and headed out.

Some weeks later, in September 1804, the Corps entered Teton Sioux territory (near present-day Pierre, South Dakota). The Tetons had earned a wicked reputation for stopping boatmen and forcing them to hand over their cargo. Armed against attack, the captains felt prepared to confront a hostile tribe. When three Teton boys

swam up to the keelboat to view the visitors, the captains told them
to convey this message: The explorers expected to have a powwow
with their chiefs.

An island was selected as a site for the council. The Corps set up
an awning, planted an American flag next to it, and unpacked gifts.
As a precaution Lewis and Clark ordered all their men, including
York, to be ready with rifles. York was needed, for he was a fine

marksman. When the chiefs arrived, there was the usual speech, gift giving, and parade. Then the Indians were given a tour of the keelboat and treated to sips of whiskey. A chief named Partisan appeared to be drunk. He said he was insulted because he hadn't received enough presents. When brought back to shore, Partisan ordered three Tetons to grab one of the expedition's boats.

York was probably close by when Clark drew his sword and warned the Tetons that he had "more medicine on board his boat than would kill twenty such nations in a day."[2] Head chief Black Buffalo immediately ordered the men to release the boat. Reacting to this disagreeable experience, Clark named the island where this took place "Bad Humored Island"—"as we were in a bad humor."[3]

To put them in a better mood, Chief Black Buffalo invited them to attend a banquet at his village. Lewis and Clark accepted for the entire Corps—and ordered all their men to carry guns. After feasting and being entertained by ten musicians with tambourines, York and the others watched a war dance staged by women waving enemies' scalps on poles.

Four days and nights with the Tetons had been nerve-wracking for everybody. Clark claimed he never slept the entire time. On September 28, after these Indians again tried and failed to hold on to one of the expedition's boats, the Corps of Discovery sailed away.

Continuing up the Missouri, the Corps passed Arikara Indian villages that had been abandoned by the few survivors of a smallpox epidemic that had killed most of their tribe.[4] The second week in October, the explorers

An Arikara

found some Arikaras camped on a large island on the river.[5]

All eyes were riveted on York, who was the focus of their attention and their admiration. According to Clark, "Those Indians were much astonished at my Servent, they never Saw a black man before, all flocked around him & examind him from top to toe."[6] The Indians thought him extraordinarily strong looking and attractive. Arikara women were intrigued by York. Although other members of the expedition enjoyed the favors of women, none were as sought after as York.

Crowds of children followed York everywhere. He was so amused that to be funny he clowned around, saying he was a wild, people-eating animal. His playfulness and sense of humor bothered Clark, who was concerned because "he Carried on the joke and made himself more turibal [terrible] than we wished him to doe."[7] However, the

Because of his color, York was the center of attention.

natives were so entranced by York that they called him "Big Medicine." The word *medicine* was adopted from English to mean "spiritual power." Clark noted, "Those people are much pleased with my black Servent."[8] He had never imagined that York would be so popular and, indeed, it was the first time that the uniqueness of his slave's skin color had made an enormous impression. The tribes they had encountered up to this time had not taken particular notice of York because they had seen persons with black skin before.

York undoubtedly enjoyed the Arikaras' attention. Here among the Indians, he could be proud of his color.

Waiting

BY THE LAST WEEK in October 1804, ice, snow, and freezing rain forced the captains to realize they had to stop traveling and wait out the winter. (They were north of present-day Bismark, North Dakota.) They decided to set up a fortified camp near the Mandans, a tribe accustomed to visitors. Mandan villages were major marketplaces where French and English traders traded guns and goods for furs, Cheyennes and Crows exchanged horses for food, and Sioux tribesmen bartered buffalo meat for corn, beans, squash, and tobacco.

When the explorers reached the Mandans, they were relieved that these Indians encouraged them to stay. Within days York helped build wooden cabins with tables, beds, and benches. In less than three weeks, Camp Fort Mandan had "two rows of huts or sheds, forming an angle where they join each other; each row containing four rooms, of 14 feet square and 7 feet high" closed in by a fence 18 feet high.[1] The camp was a mile away from the round, earth-covered lodges of the Mandans. This was to be the explorers' home for almost five months, from November 1804 to April 1805.

Once again York was the sensation. The natives crowded around him because of his black skin. Chief One Eye, a Hidatsa who lived nearby, insisted upon examining him closely. He "spit on his finger and rubbed the skin expecting to wash off the paint." When One Eye declared that York "was not a painted man," all the Indians decided that York was "great medicine."[2] They attributed sacred power to him because of his skin color. His huge, muscular body and unusual features added to his impressive appearance.

A Mandan village

The fort was frequently crowded with Mandans and their neighbors, the Hidatsas, who came to view York and to watch camp activities. They were very amused when the expedition members relaxed by jigging and square dancing to the tunes of a fiddle. The Indians were so intrigued by the skips, twirls, leaps, kicks, and bounces and by the unique sound of the strings that they invited the Corps to dance at their villages. Clark recalled New Year's Day, 1805: "I ordered my black Servent to Dance which amused the Croud Verry much, and Somewhat astonished them, that So large a man should be active."[3]

The Indians also staged dances. The entire Corps watched a buffalo dance that lasted three days. Warriors wore the heads and skins of buffalo as they stomped to the rhythms of rattles and drums, hoping their sounds and steps would attract buffalo herds. Their dancing was not just a pastime; it was their way of praying for good hunting. Buffalo were vital to the tribe's survival. The animals furnished not only meat, but also skins used for boats and clothes, sinews for ropes, and bones for hammers, rakes, and an array of other tools.

The winter was brutally cold. The river had such a thick surface of solid ice that buffalo herds galloped across without breaking through. When the temperature registered forty-two degrees below zero, standing guard outside the fort was limited to half-hour turns to prevent frostbite.

Despite the deep freeze, colder than anyone in the Corps had ever experienced, buffalo hunts took place in order to satisfy the men's enormous appetites for meat. On December 7 York went on a hunt with Clark and fourteen others in below-zero cold. The group killed

Mandan buffalo dance

A Hidatsa village

ten buffalo, then butchered and carried the beef of five buffalo back to the fort. The next day York went off with a group to retrieve the five carcasses that they had not hauled away. They were baffled because the buffalo they had shot could not be found. The men had to go back to the fort empty handed. York must have remembered this excursion for a long time because parts of his skin froze, causing him to suffer from a case of frostbite.

The mystery of the disappearing dead animals was soon explained by the Indians. According to custom, anyone could claim and take a killed buffalo if it didn't have an arrow sticking in its hide. Bullets didn't count! Therefore the shot animals were free to be taken by anyone, and so the prized game had been carried away.[4]

During another hunt York and all the others spent a night sleeping on top of snow under a makeshift tent of freshly skinned buffalo hides. Each man shivered under his own blankets. The temperature registered at ten degrees below zero.

Notwithstanding the bitter weather, hunts continued. One time York and other hunters walked thirty miles on Missouri River ice tracking game, then trudged through land where the snow was knee deep. They were chilled to the bone. Even their buckskin clothing froze. That the Mandans were able to endure cold without a show of suffering was a source of amazement to them all.[5]

White traders who lived among these Indians visited the fort. A French Canadian named René Jusseaume, who had stayed among the Mandans for fifteen years, was welcomed and hired by Captain Lewis as an interpreter. Jusseaume moved into the fort with his wife and two children. Although the captains were irritated by this man's unpleasant personality, they tolerated him because they needed him. He spoke the Mandan language, could explain tribal customs, and could brief them about the local chiefs.

Toussaint Charbonneau was another visitor. This French-Canadian fur trader was a temperamental ruffian who had lived among the

Buffalo hunting in winter

neighboring Hidatsa and Mandan Indians for five years. He, too, qualified as an interpreter because he spoke French and Hidatsa and knew a few words of English.

Charbonneau was accompanied by two teenage wives, Sacagawea, who was expecting a baby, and another girl, whose name was never recorded. Both had been kidnapped from their tribe, the Shoshoni, by a Hidatsa raiding party about four years before. Sacagawea was eleven or twelve years old at that time. The Hidatsas had sold both girls to Charbonneau, who, according to reports, already owned several other young women.

A pretty Mandan girl

There was nothing unique about buying many wives. Indians had been selling male and female slaves for centuries. Slaves were captured enemies or were bought from other tribes. Enslaved Indian girls were tempting "merchandise" purchased by many white traders and trappers. The payment could be furs, guns, or the exchange of a healthy horse for one sound slave. Charbonneau had bargained and bartered for his brides. According to some reports, he won at least one girl as a result of a gambling game with her kidnappers.[6]

As soon as Charbonneau was hired by Lewis and Clark as an interpreter, he moved into a hut inside Fort Mandan with his two wives. Like Jusseaume, he was disagreeable, and so filled with self-importance that he nearly lost his job after he announced the following rules for himself:

He would not have to stand guard.
If miffed with any man, he would return home whenever he pleased.

He would decide upon the amount of provisions he wanted to carry for himself.[7]

His nervy demands did not sit well with the captains, and they told him that they could very well do without him. When he realized he could lose his job, Charbonneau meekly apologized and agreed to perform all duties assigned to him.

This unlikable egotist was probably allowed to join the expedition only because Sacagawea would accompany him. She spoke the Shoshoni language. Therefore, she'd be able to talk to her tribal chiefs and ask them to supply horses for the Corps. Horses were needed to help carry men and provisions over the Rockies.

On February 11 Sacagawea gave birth to a baby boy, Jean Baptiste, nicknamed Pomp. No one seemed concerned about having a young girl and her infant son accompany them into the unknown. In addition to her usefulness as an interpreter, she charmed everyone with her gentle, sweet ways. Charbonneau did not bring his other wife with him. No one knows what ever became of her.

Because Sacagawea was with the Corps, York was no longer the sole slave on the Lewis and Clark expedition. Despite their slave status, both would prove vital to the expedition's success.

Into the Unknown

WHEN THE RIVER ICE broke up in March, the Corps prepared to leave. Before taking off, York helped pack a huge assortment of items for President Jefferson. Three cages contained six live animals that easterners had never seen—one prairie dog, one grouse, and four magpies. One trunk and four boxes were filled with buffalo robes, bows, arrows, skins, horns, animal bones, dried plants, insect specimens, samples of soil, maps, letters, and detailed descriptions of Indian tribes—all to feed Jefferson's insatiable appetite for information. There was also an assortment of articles that Clark sent to his own home. These included plant and mineral specimens, a Mandan woman's shirt, four pairs of moccasins, leggings of antelope skin, bighorn sheep horns, and three kinds of plums (for "Sister Clark"). Joseph Field, a recruit from Kentucky, sent a spoon made from the horn of a mountain ram to his father.

York was allowed to include two Mandan buffalo robes as gifts, one for his wife and the other for his friend Ben, a slave whom Clark freed in 1802 but who still worked for him.

A decorated Indian buffalo robe was to be given to a slave woman who had not seen her husband for more than a year! It was a gift

A painted Mandan buffalo robe

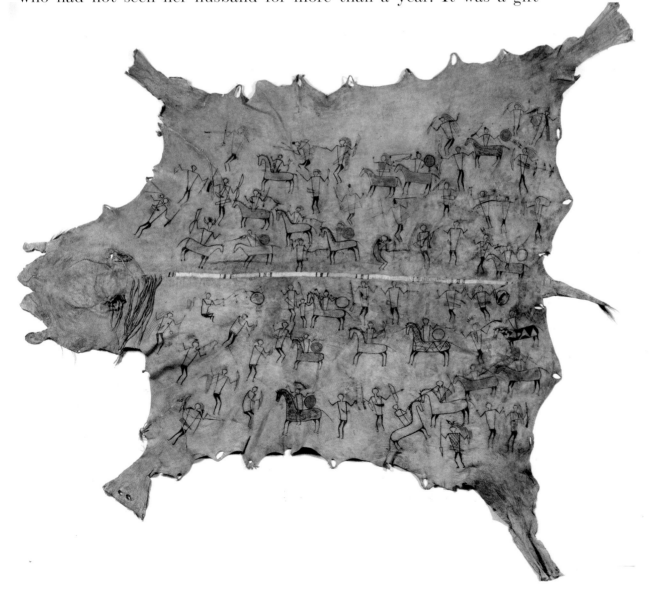

that could be cherished not only because it was unique and it could keep her warm, but most of all because it meant that York was thinking of her and loved her. This was his way of communicating with his wife, for neither of them knew how to read and write. The cargo would be shipped by the expedition's keelboat to St. Louis, then sent overland to Washington and Louisville. Items for the Clarks, York's wife, and other gift recipients were sent overland and delivered to Jonathan Clark.

To increase their capacity for carrying food, supplies, and gifts, especially because the keelboat would be leaving them for St. Louis, the captains needed to add more boats. York worked with others felling cottonwood trees and making six dugout canoes from their trunks.

When the keelboat headed out for St. Louis on April 7, 1805, the six new canoes and their two pirogues headed west. The party numbered thirty-three: the two captains, three sergeants, two interpreters, twenty-three privates, Sacagawea, her infant, and York. They were about to enter lands unknown to them where dangers could be terrifying, where, many supposed, vicious beasts and warlike Indians could kill them. Yet "not a whisper or murmur of discontent" was heard. Everyone acted "in unison and with the most perfect harmony."[1]

They passed through treeless plains (in present-day Montana) where huge herds of deer, elk, antelope, and buffalo could be seen in every direction. There were sounds York had never heard before—whistling swans and whooping cranes. The howls of wolves, the growls of grizzlies, the bellows of buffalo, and the bangs of beavers whacking water with their tails added to nature's western symphony.

After a month, scenery changed dramatically. The men found themselves walled in by sandstone cliffs that were hundreds of feet high. Wind and weather had sculpted the cliffs into gigantic, grotesque shapes.[2] The men had never dreamed that a landscape of this kind could exist. The river was so swift and the wind so fierce

York saw fantastic cliffs while traveling on the Missouri River.

that York and the other men worked hard moving the boats upstream, away from rapids and rocks.

Everyone passed a place where mounds of buffalo bodies gave off a revolting stench. Indians killed these animals by driving them over a cliff, then butchered as much meat as they could carry, leaving the remainder to rot. Wolves feasting on the carcasses made the scene a ghastly sight.

After four days beneath cliffs, the Corps sailed through treeless plains, thick with thousands of buffalo. In some places when they landed to set up camp on shore, the animals jammed together body to body and refused to budge. York and the others had "to club them out of their way."[3]

In June the explorers reached the junction of two rivers. They didn't know which of the two was a continuation of the Missouri. Captain Lewis set out on foot with a party of four to investigate the north fork.[4] Captain Clark with York and four others proceeded by boat through narrow gorges and swift waters. Driving rains chilled their bodies and soaked their skins. Although exhausted, they were kept awake at night by cold.

The river was often dangerous.

When Clark's group returned to meet Lewis's group and compare reactions to the two forks in the river, the captains decided to chance the river that Clark's group had investigated, because its clear waters could mean its source came from the western mountains.

Before setting out again, York helped make a cache, a place to bury equipment that could be uncovered and used on their return trip. A round, six-foot-deep hole was dug to bury tools, guns, food, animal traps, bear skins, beaver skins, clothes, and "all the heavy baggage wich we could possibly do without."[5] The men also hid one of their boats under a heap of branches and driftwood. Then Lewis, with a small party, hiked ahead to find the falls, and York, as part of Clark's group, rode the river.

The Great Falls

AFTER TWO DAYS of hard hiking, Lewis's group reached the Great Falls, "the grandest sight . . . the river was one continued sene of rapids and cascades . . . and the Clifts still retained their perpendicular structure and were from 150 to 200 feet high."[1] Clark's party joined them there.

The Great Falls was a wonder to behold, but a worry to confront. Clark feared the men were "about to enter on the most perilous and difficult part of our Voyage."[2] They would have to hike and haul six heavy canoes and more than a ton of gear around the falls. To lug these canoes overland, they built crude wagons with sturdy wheels made from nearby cottonwood trees. York carried as much baggage on his back as he could shoulder—probably more than anybody else, because in addition to his own belongings he bore an additional burden, most of Clark's gear. The journey around the Great Falls began on June 21, 1805.

Indians at the Mandan villages had briefed them to expect just one waterfall and only half a mile of portage (carrying boats and supplies). Instead, they faced five waterfalls and eighteen miles of backbreaking portage. It was agonizing. The men were "limping from soreness of their feet, others faint and unable to stand for a few minutes."[3] Sun scorched them. Rains soaked them. Mosquitoes plagued them. Rattlesnakes threatened them, and the fright and sight of bears unnerved them so that, whenever they stopped to camp, they slept with guns at their sides.

The eighth day they were at the Great Falls, a violent storm brought huge hailstones that could bloody their heads and ferocious winds that could blow them into the river. For safety from wind and hail, Clark found shelter in a ravine and led Sacagawea, with her baby and Charbonneau, into it.

York had been off hunting when the storm started. He rushed back to be near Clark and became frantic when he could not find him. Despite heavy hail and howling winds, York clambered up slopes and over cliffs looking for Clark. When he finally found his master, Clark had just scrambled out of a ravine to the top of a hill and he had pulled Sacagawea, her baby, and Charbonneau up with him. The ravine quickly filled with water "10 feet deep with a torrent which [was] turrouble to behold."[4]

Clark commented that York had been "greatly agitated, for our wellfar [welfare]."[5] York had voluntarily risked his own life to search for his master. To celebrate their reunion—and warm themselves as they waited out the storm—the group drank "spirits" that York carried in his canteen.

It took twelve days to go the eighteen miles around the five Great Falls. The Corps then set up camp and spent two weeks recuperating from the ordeal. York was very sick the first day. When he regained strength, he began again to look after his master's comfort. He also joined others hunting game, butchering meat, cooking meals, and making deerskin outfits to replace clothes that dampness had rotted into rags.

When the Corps headed out, everyone hiked along the shore, except for a few men in the boats, until they were stopped short by awesome mountains. Lewis and Clark realized that the men would not be able to bear the weight of their baggage while they climbed. The mountains were higher than any they had ever seen before. The

On the Missouri River, nineteen hundred miles above St. Louis

Corps had to have horses to carry their supplies. Lewis once again worried, "If we do not find them [the Shoshonis] or some other nation who have horses I fear the successfull issue of our voyage will be very doubtfull."[6]

There was "no game of any kind in the mountains."[7] Locating the Shoshonis seemed the best hope of replenishing the Corps's dwindling supply of food. And they realized they needed Indians' guidance going through mountains that could entrap and kill them. According to Lewis, not finding the Shoshonis "would defeat the expedition altogether."[8]

On July 18 Clark hiked ahead of the boats with York and two of his soldiers to look for Shoshonis. They had not seen a native for months—not since their stay with the Mandans the previous April. They spent five days searching for signs of other human beings.

Finding the Shoshonis

It was Lewis who found the Indians, thanks to Sacagawea. When they reached the Three Forks, where the river split in three directions, she cried out that this was the precise spot where she had been kidnapped five years before.

Because Sacagawea recognized landmarks and could speak Shoshoni, it's hard to understand why Lewis did not take her with him when he scouted ahead looking for her tribe. The explanation may be that Lewis believed all females were flighty creatures who could not be relied upon to act responsibly.[1] Lewis went off with two soldiers and an interpreter who did not know the language.

When Lewis saw an Indian on horseback, he was "overjoyed at the sight of this stranger."[2] To reassure him, Lewis gave his gun to one of his men and walked toward the Indian. To lure him, Lewis held out beads, a mirror, and other trinkets. Despite this, the Indian was not about to befriend a man who might be an enemy, and he turned his horse and rode away.

It took another two days of searching the wilderness before Lewis came upon three Indian women who had been gathering roots for food. The frightened women cowered as though they expected to be killed or captured. They had known about other females who, like Sacagawea, had been kidnapped and enslaved. Lewis gave the women gifts and, after he dabbed their cheeks with red paint as a sign of peace, they agreed to lead Lewis and his followers to their camp.

On the way, sixty mounted warriors rode toward them. Lewis set aside his fears, put down his gun, picked up a flag, and walked toward them. When the women leading Lewis showed the men the gifts they had just received, the warriors became unusually friendly. Lewis wrote, "They embraced me very affectionately . . . . We were all carresed and besmeared with their grease and paint till I was heartily tired of the national hug."[3] However, these greasy embraces were worthwhile because contact had been made, and these Indians brought the group to their chief, Cameahwait, who was at their camping grounds.

Lewis and his men entered an old tipi. Seated in a circle, they were ready for a powwow with Chief Cameahwait. Lewis was barefoot and told his men to take off their shoes; the Indians pulled off their own moccasins before passing a peace pipe. This was a Shoshoni custom, which Lewis thought symbolized "the misery of going barefoot forever if they are faithless in their words, a penalty by no means light to those who rove over the thorny plains of their country."[4]

Lewis indicated with gestures that his men were famished. Cameahwait apologized for providing a meal of flour and dried berry cakes. He explained that the Shoshonis were very poor because enemies raided their camps and attacked them whenever they hunted.

The Indians seemed at ease until Lewis told them that more white men were expected to arrive. That news made them very agitated and frightened. The Indians suspected that Lewis was anticipating reinforcements to help attack them.

Lewis realized he had to assure the Shoshonis that the white men who were coming were peaceful. He led them to the very place where he expected to find Clark's group waiting for him. Clark was not there! That alarmed the Shoshonis and dismayed Lewis, who realized he had to act at once to regain the tribe's trust. He gave his rifle to Cameahwait, and his three men gave their guns to the Indians, saying in simple sign language that the Shoshonis could shoot them if they didn't believe in them. Suspicion seemed to simmer down, yet everyone was unnerved.

A Shoshoni warrior

At night Cameahwait slept at Lewis's side—too close for comfort—but near enough so that each could be alert to the other's moves.

An Important Meeting

LEWIS REALIZED he had to allay the natives' fears or they would pack up and leave. Then all would be lost. The Corps faced frightening mountains. Without a Shoshoni guide and Shoshoni horses, the expedition could not go on.

York came to mind! Lewis remembered how the Arikara and Mandan Indians had reacted to this black man. They had been excited to see him, at first because of his unfamiliar dark skin and then because of his huge size and strength. York had been a sensation. The Shoshonis should surely want to see him.

Lewis piqued the chief's curiosity by describing York, who would arrive with Clark. Here was a human being of a type they had never seen—"a man perfectly black, whose hair was short and curled"—and so they were greatly impressed by the description.[1] Black was a sacred color to many tribes, including the Shoshonis. They took their chances, waiting for York's arrival in Clark's boat.[2]

Within a short time the boat docked and York stood ashore.[3] Shoshoni warriors who succeeded in battle blackened their faces with charcoal to show that they had fought bravely and successfully. York's entire body was naturally black. A color that usually meant "powerless slave" meant "powerful warrior" for the Shoshonis. Once again, York became "big medicine," an irresistible attraction. He was also "big medicine" for the others in the Corps, because his black skin helped make their white skins welcome.

Sacagawea also arrived with Clark and played a dramatic role. When she entered camp, she danced, and she rushed through a crowd to hug a childhood friend. Then, when called into a tipi to translate Shoshoni, she burst into tears, threw a blanket over Chief Cameahwait (as a greeting), and cried out that he was her brother! Even though he hadn't seen her for five years, the chief did not display emotion. However, he was probably pleased to see Sacagawea—and he did need her to translate his wishes for guns, so that the tribe could hunt without fearing enemies.[4]

A warrior who succeeded in battle would blacken his face.

The Shoshonis needed guns; the Corps had to have horses. Bargaining began. Translations took place in three time-consuming stages:

1. Sacagawea translated Shoshoni into Hidatsa.
2. Her husband, Charbonneau, translated Hidatsa into French.
3. Interpreter Labiche translated French into English. (Lewis had hired him in St. Charles because, in addition to French and English, Labiche spoke several native languages.)

Then this process was reversed: English to French to Hidatsa to Shoshoni.

Everyone was on edge. Lewis declared that he needed Shoshoni help "to penetrate the country as far as the ocean to the west of them . . . and find out a more direct way to bring merchandise to them [the Shoshonis]." In order to do so, he emphasized that the Corps needed horses to transport them and their baggage, and, in addition, "a pilot to conduct us through the mountains was also necessary." Cameahwait asked for guns in return for his help. Lewis explained that "he was sorry to find it must yet be some time before they could be furnished with firearms," but he promised to supply the Shoshonis with weapons after the expedition was completed.[5]

The prospect of trade goods and the promise of guns was so tempting for Cameahwait that he assigned a guide, called Toby, and supplied horses for the Corps's trip across the mountains.

Sacagawea, as the chief's sister and as interpreter of Shoshoni, had eased the way for the explorers' acceptance among the natives, but so had York. His imposing presence had also been of vital importance. The Shoshonis' desire to see this man with black skin and curly hair proved an effective lure that kept them with Lewis, waiting for Clark's party. If the Shoshonis had left, the Corps would never have received the horses they urgently needed to continue west.

Onward!

York would travel over these snow-covered Bitterroot Mountains.

THE SHOSHONIS PROVIDED the expedition with twenty-nine horses; "nearly all [had] sore backs, and several [were] pore, and young."[1] Toby, their guide, led them over the terrifying Bitterroot Mountains, the most dangerous part of the Rockies.

Although most of the Corps traveled on horseback, York had to hike. Trudging through snow and ice was excruciating. After two days his feet were so sore and painful that he was allowed to ride a horse—more comfortable, but more frightening. He watched other horses slip on ice, stumble in snow, and slide down slopes. Some of the animals that fell were hurt so badly, they could no longer carry a rider or supplies. Nevertheless, most were rescued and hobbled behind the group—to be eaten, in case the men faced starvation.

The Corps had started across the Bitterroots on August 30, 1805. After five days of bitter cold and gnawing hunger, the men descended into a valley (near present-day Sula, Montana), where they came upon a huge camp of Flathead Indians who, like the Shoshonis, owned hundreds of horses. The captains immediately staged their traditional performance: speeches about the Great Father in Washington

who takes care of all his "red children," gift giving of medals and trinkets to show generosity. The hungry Corps was fed a meal of roots and berries. Comforted by food and heartened by the warm welcome, the Corps set up camp near the Flatheads. They stayed for three days.

York was again the center of attention. He was such an astonishing sight that all the Indians crowded around him. The Flatheads assumed that every inch of his body had been smeared with charcoal to glorify him as a great warrior. In their eyes he was the bravest man in the entire Corps.[2]

Their high regard for York probably strengthened the captains' success as horse traders. The Flatheads gave eleven of their sound horses in exchange for an assortment of trade goods and seven of the Corps's run-down, worn-out horses.

A week after leaving the Flatheads, the expedition camped in the Bitterroots by a creek they called Traveler's Rest, where everyone did rest for a few days. Then they experienced a nightmare of mountain crossings. They rode on narrow ledges and steep peaks through drenching rains, heavy sleet, and blinding snow. They spent nights soaking wet, trying to sleep on beds of snow and pillows of ice. York, as personal servant in charge of seeing that Clark was comfortable, could do nothing to comfort his master. Clark feared his feet would freeze in his moccasins, for he declared that he was as wet and cold as he had ever been in his life.[3]

To stave off starvation, the men ate twenty pounds of candles, drank drafts of bear grease, and then reluctantly butchered some of their horses. York pushed ahead with his master and five others, trying in vain to find game. Clark named one of their campsites "Hungry Creek, as at that place we had nothing to eat."[4]

September 20, 1805: The group finally emerged from the Rocky Mountains into a broad, level valley where they came upon lodges occupied by unusual-looking Indians who inserted shells or beads through their nostrils. The tribe was called *Nez Percé*, meaning "pierced noses" in French.[5]

These Indians hadn't seen white men, although they undoubtedly knew white men existed. However, they'd never heard of a black-skinned man. According to Lewis and Clark, the Indians greeted them in a friendly manner. But, according to one Nez Percé account, when the expedition appeared, most of the Indians wanted to kill the white strangers. The Nez Percé changed their minds as soon as they saw York, who seemed fierce to them. "If we kill these others [the white men]," they supposedly said, "the black man will surely kill us."[6] If this was so, York's presence may have saved the expedition from attack. In any case, York was the big attraction. The Indians stood in a ring around him, reaching out their hands to touch him. They could not believe that his body had not been painted. Some of the women were told "to wash the black off his face."[7]

York's presence could explain why the Nez Percés were cordial. When the Nez Percés couldn't wash off the blackness, they were awed by his presence. They honored him and called him "Black Indian"—a term that classified York with them rather than with the "whites." Had it not been for York, Indians might have had second thoughts about welcoming the white strangers.

Shooting Rapids

AFTER NEARLY TWO MONTHS of suffering, the Corps emerged from the mountains onto plains and camped near the Clearwater River. Everyone looked forward to sailing once again. According to the Nez Percés, they could reach the Pacific Ocean by waterways within a week. Although everyone was "weakened and much reduced in flesh as well as strength" and "nearly all men sick," they worked hard hollowing tree trunks to make canoes.[1] They also branded all their horses and left the animals with the Nez Percés, who promised to take care of them until the Corps returned from the great ocean.

On October 7, 1805, the men lowered five new canoes into the Clearwater River, expecting clear sailing. The first day out one of the canoes hit a rock and sprang a leak. The next day another canoe capsized and sank. Fortunately, the water was so shallow that the men were able to wade to shore. After shooting some hair-raising rapids, Toby quit and headed back to the Shoshonis, without giving notice or collecting his pay. He was probably frightened by the Corps's daring and recklessness.

Three days of paddling, poling, and plummeting down falls on the Clearwater were followed by six days on the Snake River, where once again sudden rapids jolted and terrified them. When not shooting rapids, they rode currents swifter "than any horse could run."[2] Time after time they faced death as wild waters pushed their canoes over sudden edges and down steep declines. Astonished Indians who watched them from land marveled that the canoes didn't crash and smash to bits, killing the riders.[3] But the Corps, in a hurry to reach the coast before winter snows, kept up their risky breakneck speed.

York saw many Indians clustered along the riverbank catching salmon as fast as they could cast their nets. The waters were jammed with salmon from spring to fall. York was witnessing a mass migration of salmon that quit the Pacific Ocean and swim up rivers to spawn.

Fishing for salmon on the Columbia River

When the Snake River led them into the Columbia River, on October 16, York viewed another incredible sight. Quantities of salmon were swimming upstream, and dead ones were floating on the water and littering the shores. At that time, only Indians knew that this took place annually when, after spending years in the Pacific Ocean, salmon enter coastal streams and rivers to lay and fertilize their eggs. Then both males and females die. The hatched fry eventually swim to the sea, to start the life cycle again.[4]

Some Indians along the river were drying salmon on huge scaffolds. This process could preserve the fish for years. At one stopover York saw enormous mounds of dried salmon that women were wrapping in fish skins. Clark counted 107 bundles of salmon, which he estimated weighed close to ten thousand pounds! But the men wanted to eat meat, not fish, and so they bought dogs from the Indians and butchered them for food.

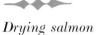

Drying salmon

All along the way Indians came up close to marvel at York, for they had never seen a black man before. York not only attracted and fascinated the Indians, he befriended them. He was such a marvelous dancer that Clark liked to show him off. He frequently ordered York to dance, knowing that natives enjoyed watching him move to music.

The natives would have been shocked had they known that this impressive dancer had been born a slave. Like York, Indians were considered inferiors by whites. Lewis and Clark's speeches implied that. During their routine powwow performances, the captains talked down to the "red children," telling them about a "white father" who would take care of them only if they "opened their ears" and followed the wishes of white men. Their words conveyed the fearsome message that Indians were powerless, inferior human beings.

*Meeting Indians
in the Northwest*

It is a wonder most Indians didn't resent the explorers and react angrily. Instead, they supplied the expedition with food, horses, and advice about passageways ahead. The expedition would have failed had it not been for Indian aid, but Indians received merely meager gifts—medals, bells, beads, thimbles, pins, wires, and other trinkets—as rewards for their lifesaving services.

The Columbia River cut through the Cascade Mountains, and again York and the others whooshed down the river, fighting to float their boats through currents "swelling, boiling & whirling in every direction."[5]

When the expedition reached calmer waters in November, the men speedily paddled toward the ocean. But their spirits were soon dampened by rain and winds that whipped the waters into waves so high it was hard to make any headway. Some of the men became so seasick that they must have wondered whether all their suffering would be worthwhile.

They camped with nothing to eat except dried salmon and nothing to drink except rainwater, for the river's water was salty and made those who drank it sick. Rain rotted clothes and bedding. Fleas tormented them. Everyone was cold, wet, weakened, and miserable.

When the river calmed down, the men proceeded on. They were deeply encouraged when they saw an Indian wearing a sailor's jacket and other natives wearing trousers, hats, and shirts that had been made back east in America or in Europe. They met Indians who spoke a few words of English, and one who knew the name of a white trader who obtained goods from ships that docked at Pacific Ocean ports. Here was sure proof that, after a year and a half of hardship, the Corps was near its goal.

On November 7, 1805, they reached "this great Pacific ocean which we had been so long anxious to see."[6]

Dampened Spirits

Sacagawea and Charbonneau can be seen in this celebratory image of the expedition at the Pacific Ocean.

ELATION AT REACHING the coast soon changed to misery. The Corps's tents were shaky and leaked. Constant rain drenched the men, soaked their bedding, and spoiled much of their food. They obviously needed to build a sturdy fort that would keep them comfortable for the entire winter. Even though a decision about locating a camp was usually made by military officers, Clark allowed the men to decide by voting. Every member of the expedition voted—including York and Sacagawea! They voiced approval for building a fort on the south side of the river, on high ground about four miles from the ocean (near present-day Astoria, Oregon). Good hunting was reportedly close by.

York was the first black person to have any kind of recorded vote in North America. Nearly sixty years before slaves in the United States would be emancipated and enfranchised, York had a say in deciding where the Corps was to have its winter quarters! York was also the first black man to cross the United States from coast to coast. Sacagawea voted too—more than a century before women or Indians were given voting rights by the United States government.

Once again York felled trees, cleared land, cut logs, and helped build Fort Clatsop. It consisted of seven huts, a parade ground, and a high, gated wall to keep out stray animals and unwanted visitors and to shelter and protect the Corps.

By Christmas Eve, after nearly three weeks of working in pouring rain, the fort was finished and the men were able to move in. Christmas morning was saluted with a discharge of guns. That was the extent of the merriment. Everyone was exhausted, as well as uncomfortable in their new close quarters. The holiday dinner was cheerless. The menu was "pore Elk, so much Spoiled that we eat it thro' mear necessity, Some Spoiled pounded fish and a fiew roots."[1]

A few days after this sorry celebration, York was "very unwell from a violent cold, and strain by carrying meat from the woods and lifting the heavy logs on the works."[2] Others, too, were sick with fever and muscle pains. On New Year's Day the men complained that there was no liquor to lift their spirits, the only beverage being "pure water."

Huddled inside their dismal rooms that were curtained by smoke from drafty chimneys, the men were aggravated by fleas. Clark wrote that everyone had "great difficulty in getting those troublesome insects out of our robes and blankets."[3] Many times the men stripped in order to scratch their bites, then smack, shake, and pick fleas off their bodies and out of their clothes. But the fleas thrived and would not give up their cozy quarters. Clark had his blankets searched and the fleas killed every day—probably the job of York, who had problems enough trying to keep flea free himself.

The gates of Fort Clatsop were open to visitors during the day but shut tight at night. Even though isolated and bored by indoor living, the men welcomed only those visitors who supplied food or female company and those who gave information about the land around them. They especially wanted to be shielded from the frequent visits of Chinook Indians, whom they disliked because some of them had pilfered knives, pipes, axes, and other of the Corps's belongings. However, the group needed the fish these poor Indians provided, and therefore they allowed them into the fort.[4]

During the Corps's miserable stay of more than four months, there were only twelve days it didn't rain, and the sky was covered with clouds six of those dry days. In addition to caring for Clark, York joined the others curing and cutting elk leather for shirts, pants, and footgear. Moccasins must have proven to be the most fascinating (or

Fort Clatsop was near Chinook lodges, like this one.

easiest) to fashion. They made **338** pairs—far more than they might ever need. But it kept them busy.

Spending time well was not a problem for the captains. They could read and write—unlike **York** and many other men of the Corps. And they had lugged along volumes for study. Although they needed to travel as lightly as possible, journals and heavy books about animals, plants, stars, and minerals were necessities, especially because the captains were anxious to learn and also to furnish detailed reports to President Jefferson. Lewis spent much of his time at Fort Clatsop studying and adding information to his journals that listed everything he could about Indian tribes, including notations about their vocabularies and descriptions about the clothing they wore and the huts they inhabited. Clark punctuated his journals with drawings of people, places, plants, and animals that had never been described in books before. He wrote notes, sketched scenes, and made maps that often used names of Corps members to mark sites. There was even a cluster of small islands in the upper Missouri River that Clark named "York's 8 Islands."

Because he was a skilled hunter, York was allowed to leave the fort's close quarters to hunt with others. They aimed for elk. The men ate boiled elk, dried elk, and smoked elk day after day, for breakfast and dinner. However, hunting wasn't always good. Instead of elk, York often came back with

Clark's sketch of a candlefish

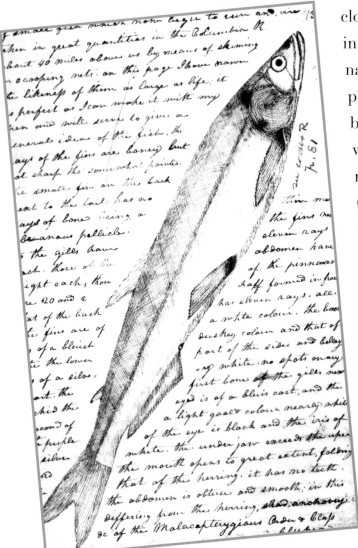

squirrels and hawks, not anyone's favorite bill of fare. Dried fish and berries purchased from the Clatsops and Chinooks filled out their menu, but the men found these foods merely tolerable.

When told by Indians that a dead whale had been washed ashore, York set out with Clark, twelve corpsmen, and an Indian guide to find it and cut some whale steaks for themselves. They hiked more than seventeen miles only to find a whale skeleton that had been picked dry of flesh. It was just a giant scaffold of bones that Clark estimated was 105 feet long.

Tillamook Indians who camped nearby had stripped the carcass. York watched them cut blubber, boil it in wooden tubs to extract whale oil, then store the oil in the whale's bladder and guts. Clark bought three hundred pounds of blubber and a few gallons of oil. Lewis called the whale meat "verry palitable and tender," but these tasty meals lasted only a few weeks.[5] Then the menu went back to tough elk, dried fish, and occasionally roasted dog.

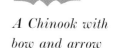

A Chinook with bow and arrow

By March everyone was anxious to leave the damp, depressing winter camp and head home. In case the Corps met disaster and didn't make it back to the East, the captains decided to leave evidence that they had journeyed across the continent. They listed the names of the Corps's men on several sheets of paper. They also stated that the group had been "sent out by the government of the U.States in May 1804 to explore the interior of the continent of North

America, did penetrate the same by way of the Missouri and Columbia rivers . . . to the Pacific Ocean."[6] The captains pasted one copy of this document on a wall in Fort Clatsop and distributed other copies to Indians who lived nearby, hoping that through trading at least one of these papers would find its way to a ship bound for the United States. "York, a black man of Captain Clark's" was included on the captains' list of the expedition's members.

After handing over Fort Clatsop as a gift to the Clatsop Indians, the captains were eager to get going. They didn't heed Indian warnings that wicked winter conditions could still kill them. They could not bear to stay at the fort another day. York packed his master's belongings and helped pack possessions and provisions that were to be loaded onto canoes.

On March 23, 1806, the group headed for home.

3. HOMEWARD BOUND

A few days after leaving Fort Clatsop, the captains heard from Indians who paddled by that there was a tragic food shortage. Indians along the river were starving. They had used up all the fish they had dried the season before, and another salmon run would not take place in the river for at least one month. This dismaying information caused "much uneasiness with respect to the future means of subsistence." It presented "a gloomy prospect" for the future. However, the expedition kept going for two reasons: They had to hurry to pick up the horses left with the Nez Percés before that tribe left for a buffalo hunt. And they could not spend weeks waiting for the salmon to appear because they had to reach the Missouri River before it froze solid and ice blocked their waterway to St. Louis.[1]

The expedition's supply of food became critically short, and Indians along the way refused to sell any provisions. Clark was so desperate that he performed tricks that might make them believe he was a magician with superhuman powers. York watched Clark hold a magnet to his pocket compass so that the compass's needle spun around. His master also changed the flame colors of their campfire by throwing an artillery match into it.[2]

These stunts frightened the Indians so much that they begged Clark to take whatever food he wanted and be gone. However, all they were able to supply were bundles of wapatoo roots. These roots had been gathered by women who jumped from canoes into chilling water that was shoulder high. They used their toes to locate and loosen the roots from the soil below, then grabbed the roots and threw them into their canoes. It was punishing work. The women had to stay "in the water for several hours even in the depth of winter," suffering from cold and exhaustion.[3]

After receiving a disappointingly small supply of these roots, Clark chose York, along with seven others, to hunt with him. They stalked game along a new river they had discovered (now called the Willamette). They shot, butchered, and dried bear, elk, and deer meat, a supply that would feed them for a short time. They felt lucky to have any food—especially after they saw starving Indians who tried to stop hunger pains by swallowing moss and gnawing on the bark of trees.

It wasn't until the end of April, when the Corps reached the junction of the Columbia and Snake Rivers, that the men met Indians willing and able to feed the Corps. Walla Walla Chief Yellept remembered meeting and enjoying the group the previous October, when the expedition was on its way west. He brought them presents of firewood and fish, and he invited the Corps to stay at his village.

The captains bought ten dogs from the tribe. Dog meat was a dish that most of the Corps relished as flavorful. (Lewis's dog, Seaman, was safe because he was a pet.) The Indians in the area did not butcher and eat dogs; nor did they keep them as pets. They used dogs as pack animals or hitched them to haul carts. Since the Corps was running short of gifts, Clark reluctantly gave up his sword plus two

hundred balls of powder to pay for the dogs.

Realizing that he had to perform some service in return for more food, this time Clark acted as a doctor. He accepted food as his fee. York most likely played the part of medical assistant, unpacking and handling medicines that the Corps used for an assortment of minor ailments, such as eye and skin irritations. Clark took great care "to give them no article which can possibly injure them [the Indians]," for he was aware that he was not a trained physician and only knew some "folk medicine."[4]

The last evening of their three-day stay with the Walla Wallas, York had a chance to show off his talents as a dancer. Although other

Some tribes used dogs as pack animals.

men of the expedition also danced, York fascinated the Indians not only because of his unusual skin color, but also because of his agility. After dancing in front of hundreds of Walla Wallas, York watched the Indians sing and dance to drumbeats. The Corps's dancing was a carefree recreation; the Indians' dancing was a way of praying, a religious ritual.

Staying with Chief Yellept had been a holiday. It was restful and helpful. The Walla Wallas provided the Corps with additional horses so that they could continue their journey overland. And they gave instructions about a shortcut for the journey ahead, to hasten their way home.

On April 30, 1806, the explorers left the Walla Wallas, "those honest friendly people," and set their sights for the Clearwater River, where they would find their friends the Nez Percés.[5]

York's Mission

RAIN, SNOW, AND HIGH WINDS kept the Corps from racing ahead. Within days the men had used up their supply of food "and had not anything for tomorrow."[1] There was no game to hunt, and there were few fish to catch. By the time they met roving bands of Nez Percés, Clark realized he had to resume doctoring and dispensing medicines to earn food. Natives used roots and dogs to pay for medical treatment.

On May 8 the explorers reached Chief Twisted Hair's Nez Percé village. Twisted Hair rounded up all but two of the horses that had been left in his care, and his men dug up the saddles and ammunition that the Corps had cached in the ground the year before.

The captains were disheartened to hear from Twisted Hair that Indian trails across the Bitterroot Range were buried under deep snow and they would freeze or starve to death unless they waited until the weather was warmer. The captains heeded the chief's warnings and waited. York helped to build a campsite, Camp Chopunnish, a few miles away from Twisted Hair's lodge. The Corps stayed there for nearly a month, from May 14 to June 10, 1806.

Everyone hoped that the enforced stay would give them the time to stockpile food to be used when going over mountains, "where hungar an Cold in their most rigorous form assail the waried traveller."[2] No one could ever forget their ordeal the year before, when they starved while crossing the Bitterroots.

Clark's services as a doctor were, again, in great demand. Patients lined up to be examined, advised, and medicated. Indians came from miles around for treatment—and to view York, always an effective magnet who drew Indians to inspect and admire him. However, although they marveled at York and appreciated Clark's medical treatments, the Indians did not bring much food. The captains resorted to giving each of their men thread, ribbons, paints, and pins to trade for roots. But the Indians were loath to give up the scant supply of food they were saving for themselves.

Lewis and Clark turned to York. Because of his popularity with natives, they thought that he might be able to buy provisions. They chose him to visit a village eight miles away and gave him trinkets to barter for food. Charbonneau went along as interpreter, and Private Jean Lepage accompanied him for security. York's bargaining skills were so effective that he brought back four bags of roots and a load of root bread. This was a great accomplishment. Even though the Indians had little to spare for themselves, York had convinced them to part with food and take trifles as payment.

York's success as a trader was so impressive that a few days after he returned, the captains sent him on another food-getting mission. This time Private Hugh McNeal accompanied him. The captains were extremely short of gifts. In addition to tin boxes and glass bottles, they gave York buttons they had cut off their own coats! Once again, York was successful. His customers accepted the needles and buttons, which they used as decorations on their clothing. The bottles and boxes were sought after items because they were made of glass or metal, not of wood, gourds, or braided grasses.

The captains were elated when York returned with three bushels of roots and bundles of root bread. York's mission was praised as "a suckcessfull voyage . . . not much less pleasing to us than the return of a good cargo to an East Indian merchant."[3] York had obtained provisions that would help the Corps survive the ordeal of the Bitterroots.

Return to St. Louis

DESPITE BEING WARNED against crossing the mountains until the snow melted, Lewis and Clark were too impatient to wait. Even though Indian guides refused to accompany them because of the dangers, the Corps headed out on horseback on June 10, 1806. This time York did not have to climb on foot. He was given a horse to ride and another horse to carry his belongings.

On June 15, 1806, the expedition started across the Bitterroots. Deep snow erased trails, but they rode ahead for two days until the snow measured "from 12 to 15 feet deep." Clark despaired, "Here was winter with all its rigors; the air was cold . . . hands and feet were benumbed . . . under these circumstances we conceived it madnes[s] in this stage of the expedition to proceed without a guide."[1] The expedition had to turn back. This was the first and only time during the expedition that the Corps was "compelled to retreat."[2]

When they got out of the mountains, the Corps met two Nez Percés who agreed to accept a fee of two guns to guide them over the

Bitterroots. On June 25 the group set out with these guides. There were steep climbs and sharp descents all day, with the cold comfort of snowy beds at night. The men were so disoriented by sky-high peaks and jutting cliffs looming over them that, were it not for the Indian guides, they could have been trapped forever. It took six days of suffering before the group emerged from mountains to meadows.

Despite the rush to return, Lewis and Clark decided to split up and spend time exploring new territory. Lewis was to follow Maria's River to its source, and Clark was to explore the Yellowstone River. They would join forces at the confluence of the Yellowstone and Missouri Rivers.

Crossing the Bitterroot Mountains was agonizing.

Clark, with York and nine other men, paddled down the Yellowstone for 636 miles. On the way York helped dig up canoes and supplies that had been cached the year before. He also hunted elk and buffalo for the men's meals. York was undoubtedly pleased that Clark named a small tributary of the Yellowstone "York's dry river." This was the second time Clark had named a place for his slave. The names of all Corps members eventually appeared on Clark's maps. On August 3 Clark's group followed the Yellowstone to its junction with the Missouri River and waited for Lewis.

Lewis and his men were taking a shortcut to the Great Falls of the

Missouri when they came upon eight Blackfeet warriors. Although suspicious of each other, they feigned friendship and camped together for the night. Lewis was awakened at daybreak by the shouts of his men. The Indians were seizing their guns! Lewis reached for his own gun. It had been taken too! One of his men stabbed an Indian in the heart— "the fellow ran about 25 steps and fell dead." Lewis shot another in the stomach.[3] The Blackfeet fled. Lewis and his men fled too—but not until they first grabbed four of the tribe's horses and some buffalo meat. They galloped away as fast as they could to distance themselves from Blackfeet encampments. This was the only time during the entire expedition that

the Corps had killed an Indian—the only time the Corps had fought Indians.

They rode day and night until they had "the unspeakable satisfaction to see our canoes" with the men Clark had left at the falls. After being told that Clark was somewhere on the Yellowstone River, they dismounted, set the horses free, then jumped into the boats.[4]

When they passed a large herd of elk, Lewis landed to hunt with his river man, Cruzatte. Lewis shot an elk, and he was taking aim at another when he was shot in the buttocks by a bullet. Cruzatte, who "can not see very well," had mistaken him for an elk.[5] When they caught up with Clark, on August 12, Lewis was a sorry sight. He lay at the bottom of his boat in agony; his wound was so painful he could barely move, but he would soon recover.

A Mandan lodge

The Corps paddled ahead for two days, until they arrived at the land of the Mandans. The explorers were delighted to be back with their friends. Charbonneau was especially pleased because the expedition ended for him here, where Lewis and Clark had first met him. He would reestablish his headquarters and resume his career as a fur trapper. Sacagawea would set up home for him and their child. The captains paid Charbonneau the exact sum of \$500.33 $\frac{1}{3}$ cents for his services.

Sacagawea had earned the heartfelt affection of everyone in the Corps. They had prized her presence and valued her help. But despite her role as a food gatherer, advisor, and Shoshoni interpreter, Sacagawea was not given any pay—after all, she was merely a woman, and only a slave!

After leaving the Mandans, the explorers speeded down the Missouri, covering up to seventy miles a day. They didn't even take time out to hunt, because they wanted to get home quickly. The Corps stopped to visit the friendly Arikaras but avoided the Tetons, who hooted at them from the shores. Clark, who remembered how troublesome that tribe had been on the way west, "determined to put up with no insults . . . [and] directed them to return with their band to their camp, that if any of them come near our camp we Should kill them certainly."[6] Proceeding down the river, the explorers took time out to smoke peace pipes with the friendly Yanktons and stopped to visit the grave of Sergeant Floyd, the Corps's only fatality.

Then, oh, the joy of greeting American traders and trappers, who were paddling their way up the river! The Corps was excited to see and speak with strangers who were not Indians. The traders and trappers were astonished to encounter the expedition. Some assumed the Corps had lost their lives in a forbidding wilderness. Others supposed they had been killed by frightful monsters, or by "wild" Indians. One trader told the men that the Corps "had been long Since given out [up] by the people of the U S Generally, and almost forgotten." Still, they learned, "The President of the U.States had yet hopes of us."[7]

On September 23, 1806, this Corps of Discovery reached St. Louis. Because the explorers had been gone for nearly two and a half years and been presumed lost, people were startled to see them. Crowds went wild. They shouted hurrahs and hailed all of the Corps members as heroes.

Since St. Louis didn't have a newspaper, the first printed announcement appeared in the *Palladium* of Frankfort, Kentucky, on October 2: "We stop the press to announce with sincere pleasure, the following HIGHLY INTERESTING INTELLIGENCE. . . . Captains Lewis and Clark are just arrived, all in the good health." On October 9 readers of the *Palladium* read, "We congratulate the

We stop the press to announce, with sincere pleasure, the following

HIGHLY INTERESTING INTELLIGENCE.

St. Louis, Sept. 23, 1806.

DEAR SIR,

Captains Lewis and Clark are just arrived, all in very good health. They left the Pacific Ocean the 23d of March last—they wintered there—They arrived there in last November : there was some American vessels there just before their arrival. They had to pack one hundred and sixty miles from the head of the Missouri to Columbia river. One of the hands, an intelligent man, tells me the Indians are as numerous on the Columbia, as the whites are in any part of the United States. They brought but one family of Indians, of the Mandan nation. They have brought several curiosities with them from the Ocean. The Indians are represented as being very peaceable! The winter was very mild on the Pacific.

I am yours, &c,

JOHN MULLANPHY.

P. S. They left St Charles May 20th, 1804, and returned there Sept. 21st 1806.

J. M.

public at large and the particular friends of Messrs. Lewis and Clark and their enterprising companions, on the happy termination of an expedition, which will, doubtles[s], be productive of incalculable commercial advantage."[8] The prospects of a flourishing fur trade, new settlements, and faster access to the Pacific Ocean trade enthralled those anxious to expand the country's wealth. The Corps's adventures, bravery, and hardships were described and extolled. Reports about the expedition's return spread across the nation as fast as messengers could carry them.

York—"that boy," "that Negro," "that slave," "that black man of Captain Clark's"—tasted fame when they arrived in St. Louis. He shared the glory and acclaim that mobs bestowed upon every member of the Lewis and Clark expedition.

4. FORGOTTEN MAN

The elation York felt upon arriving in St. Louis was short-lived. At first Clark permitted him to mingle among people and tell them true tales about the expedition's adventures. But when he resumed his full-time role as personal servant, he had to remain by his master's side. Then interest in this black man faded fast, and his easy contact with white people ended. York had to realize, once again, that he was totally a slave, considered to be inferior to every white person. His skin color marked him indelibly as an underling.

Although York had been named as a member of the Corps at Camp Wood and was also listed on papers the captains had left at Fort Clatsop, when Lewis gave the War Department his official roster of men who had been to the Pacific and back, York was not on the list. As a slave he was not counted; it was as though he did not count. Sacagawea and her baby weren't listed either. Even Sergeant Floyd, who had died in 1804, and Charbonneau, whom Lewis looked down upon as "a man of no peculiar merit," were included in the list

An American fort near an Indian encampment

of twenty-nine men who had accompanied Lewis and Clark and had undergone the "fatigues and painful sufferings" of the expedition. Their praiseworthy accomplishments entitled them to the "warmest approbation and thanks" and to money and land.[1]

The government rewarded each enlisted man on the list with double pay and 320 acres of land. Lewis and Clark each received double pay and 1600 acres of land. Because he was a slave, York was not eligible for money or land.

On October 10 the expedition disbanded and left St. Louis. Imagine how elated York was to see his parents and greet the plantation slaves—and how overjoyed he was when he was given permission to visit his wife who, fortunately, was still owned by the neighbor. The sole communication his wife had received from him had been the Mandan buffalo robe he had been allowed to send to her.

York set out with Lewis and Clark to see President Jefferson in

Washington. Although the explorers had not found a direct waterway to the Pacific Ocean, Clark felt confident that the expedition did discover "the best rout[e] which does exist across the continent of North America."[2] Well dressed and carefully groomed, as a gentleman's servant should be, York attended to his master and watched passively as mobs hailed the captains as heroes and prominent people held receptions to celebrate their accomplishments.

As rewards for the expedition, Clark was made a brigadier general and Indian agent for the West and Lewis became governor of the Louisiana Territory. Both men were obligated to make St. Louis their headquarters. Clark moved to St. Louis in 1808, taking York and some other household slaves with him.

For York, leaving Kentucky was agonizing, for he would no longer be near his wife. York's wife had to remain with her master. If York and his wife had children—no one knows if that was so—the children would stay with the mother and be the neighbor's property, too. Black couples who were separated from each other had no choice but to accept owners' decisions to nullify slave marriages. That York could not abide by this cruel rule ruined his relationship with his master.

Clark surely should have realized the importance of a husband-wife relationship. Shortly after returning from the expedition, he had courted sixteen-year-old Julia Hancock. In 1808 they married, and the couple settled in St. Louis. Clark was a loving, devoted husband who relished having Julia by his side. However, he knew that slave marriages were not legal and not binding, and he was not one to defy customary slaveholders' attitudes.

Clark believed himself to be a kind, considerate slave owner when he gave York permission to visit his wife for four or five weeks. However, he became angry when York overstayed his leave and didn't return to St. Louis for close to six months. Then he was enraged to hear York declare that he preferred being sold to another master who lived near his wife's owner rather than stay with Clark. Clark was

*Clark could
have sold York
at an auction
like this one.*

furious about York's attitude. He considered it defiant, disobedient, and disloyal, and he vented his temper in letters to his brother Jonathan. "I am determined not to sell him [York] to gratify him," he wrote, " . . . if any attempt is made by York to run off, or refuse to provorm [perform] his duty as a Slave, I wish him Sent to New Orleans and Sold, or hired out to Some Severe master untill he thinks better of Such Conduct."[3]

Clark had spent his entire life with York. He never imagined that York would ever want to be permanently separated from him. That York's desire for his wife was more important than loyalty to his master angered and bewildered Clark. His slave not only refused to submit to his will but also dared to request either being sold to another master or given his freedom. Clark resented the self-esteem York had gained as a result of his contributions to the expedition's success. Clark complained to his brother that "York . . . has got such a notion about freedom and his emence [immense] Service [during the expedition] that I do not expect he will be of much Service to me again. . . . I do not expect much from him as long as he has a wife in Kenty [Kentucky]."[4]

York was no longer a delightful, dedicated personal servant. Clark found him to be "of very little Service" and "insolent and Sulky." He resorted to the whip and "gave him a Severe trouncing" at least once.[5] The close relationship between a proud owner and a devoted slave ended. In 1809 York spent a short time in jail, for unexplained reasons. Perhaps Clark put him there as punishment for rebelliousness. Even though York had been his lifelong companion, Clark felt compelled to follow a basic rule for slaveholders: that a master, as a superior being, was obligated to punish any slave who was defiant or disobedient.

Distraught, Clark asked Lewis's advice about York. Lewis counseled him not to sell or free York, but to hire him out to another master for a year. Perhaps that would ease the tension. Clark followed Lewis's advice and hired York out for one year to a Mr. Young, who lived in Louisville. Fortunately, in Louisville he would be near his wife. Unfortunately, according to a letter Clark received from a nephew, Young was mean and "misused" York, and York "appear[ed] wretched."[6]

In 1811, when York learned that his wife had to move with her master far away to Natchez, Mississippi, he despaired, for he doubted if he would ever be able to see her again.

IT WOULD BE WONDERFUL to end a true story with a happy ending. According to some fanciful accounts, York escaped to freedom and spent the rest of his life living contentedly in the Rocky Mountains among the Crow Indians, where he was honored as one of their chiefs. Other fictitious versions relate that Clark gave York his freedom in 1806, as a reward for his valuable contribution to the two-and-a-half-year, eight-thousand-mile Lewis and Clark expedition. How fine it would feel to be sure that York lived happily ever after. But that was not to be.

In 1810 Clark allowed York to deliver freight in Louisville by means of a two-horse wagon. He had found him useless as a personal servant and did not want him around. Five years later York was still in Louisville, working as a wagoner in a freighting business owned by the Clark family. Eventually—in 1816 or later, at least ten years after the expedition's return—Clark freed York and provided him with six horses and a wagon for hauling goods between Nashville, Tennessee, and Richmond, Kentucky. But as a free black competing for customers against white workers, York did poorly in business. He struggled to support himself for years, until he died—barely noticed, date unknown.

It is sad that York died unrecognized for his role in the Lewis and Clark expedition. He deserves high praise, for without his presence the Corps of Discovery might have failed. York acted as a peaceful passport to Indians. At first York was just a great curiosity. Then he became "Big Medicine" when Indians assumed his color indicated spiritual powers. His importance mounted when tribes praised him as "Black Indian" and "Brave Warrior," for to them his blackness marked him as a great person.

This "personal servant" had risked his own life when he searched for Clark during a frightening storm. It was York who traded trifles for urgently needed food to help the expedition survive. Nevertheless, York became but an obscure shadow in history who did not receive the high regard, financial rewards, and many praises we now know he deserved.

Today there is increasing
recognition of York's
contributions to the Lewis
and Clark Expedition.
This statue, shown
against the Bitterroot
Mountains, was
commissioned for the
bicentennial and created
by the African-American
sculptor Ed Hamilton.

Endnotes

1. The Early Years

1. Freed slaves, called "free persons of color," were allowed surnames.
2. As late as 1844, some southern states imposed the death penalty on slaves convicted for the second time of trying to learn to read and write.
3. According to Thomas Jefferson, thirty thousand slaves had fled from Virginia. During the Revolutionary War, many slaves ran away to Canada, Florida, and to Indian territory. Lord Dunmore, Virginia's royal governor, urged slaves to fight in the British army. He proclaimed, "All indentured servants, Negroes, and others . . . [would be] . . . free if they are able and willing to bear arms and join his Majesty's troops." Lord Dunmore lured about eight hundred blacks to fight with the British. They included one large group, trained by redcoat officers, called the "Royal Ethiopian Regiment." These black soldiers, who sported sashes with the slogan "Liberty to Slaves," would have been shocked to know that Lord Dunmore had not given any of his own fifty-seven slaves their freedom! See Joy Hakim, *History of U.S.* (New York: Oxford University Press, 1999), book 3, p. 121.
4. George Rogers Clark was an outstanding Revolutionary War hero. After the war, Congress gave him a standing ovation.

Moving West

1. Many people were disturbed by the idea of enslaving human beings, yet they accepted slavery as an age-old fact of life. After all, fathers, grandfathers, friends, and neighbors owned slaves. And slave labor not only existed all over the world, but had been practiced since biblical times. In the South slavery was required for plantation prosperity. It was called a "peculiar institution" and "a necessary evil."
2. Robert B. Betts, *In Search of York* (Boulder, Colo.: Colorado Associated University Press, 1985), p. 92.
3. *Ibid.*, p. 192.
4. That took place in 1786, just a year after the family moved to Kentucky.
5. James J. Holmberg, *Dear Brother: Letters of William Clark to Jonathan Clark* (New Haven, Conn.: Yale University Press, 2002), p. 273.
6. Betts, p. 85.

One Black Man

1. Donald Jackson, *Letters of the Lewis and Clark Expedition 1783–1854* (Urbana, Ill.: University of Illinois Press, 1962), p. 60.
2. *Ibid.*, p. 57. Clark expressed himself well, despite his odd spellings. For example, the name of the Indian tribe *Sioux* appeared in his writings as *Sous, Shoe, Shois,* and in twenty other different ways.
3. *Ibid.*
4. *Ibid.*, p. 112.
5. Cutright, Paul Russell, *Lewis and Clark: Pioneering Naturalists* (Urbana, Ill.: University of Illinois Press, 1969), p. 35.

2. Heading West

1. Bernard DeVoto, ed., *The Journals of Lewis and Clark* (Boston: Houghton Mifflin, 1953), p. 1.
2. Jackson, p. 11.
3. *Ibid.*, p. 254.
4. Betts, p. 11.
5. *Ibid.*

Whippings and Powwows

1. Reuben Thwaites, ed., *Original Journals of the Lewis and Clark Expedition* (New York: Dodd, Mead, 1904–5), vol. 7, p. 30.
2. DeVoto, p. 7.
3. www.pbs.org/lewisandclark/inside, p. 1.
4. Jackson, p. 123.
5. DeVoto, pp. 21–22.
6. John Bakeless, *Lewis and Clark: Partners in Discovery* (New York: William Morrow, 1947), p. 47.
7. Jackson, p. 203.

The First Winter

1. Bakeless, p. 57.
2. James P. Ronda, *Lewis and Clark Among the Indians* (Lincoln, Nebr.: University of Nebraska Press, 1984), p. 33.
3. Bakeless, p. 69.
4. Smallpox was a disease carried to the New World from Europe.
5. Unlike the Tetons, the Arikaras were anxious to be hospitable. At powwows, passing around swigs of whiskey was meant to put Indians in a good mood. Much to the explorers' surprise, the Arikaras refused to drink because they knew about the effects of alcohol from French traders. Their chiefs said, "[The explorers] are no friends or we would not give them [liquor] what makes them fools." www.pbs.org/lewisandclark/archive/idx_jou.html.
6. DeVoto, p. 49.
7. *Ibid.*, p. 52.
8. *Ibid.*

Waiting

1. Cutright, p. 108.
2. Betts, p. 19.
3. DeVoto, p. 75.

4. Some diaries report that Lewis, not Clark, conducted this hunt.
5. Cutright, p. 111.
6. According to Stephen Ambrose, Charbonneau won the girls in a bet with the Hidatsa warriors who had captured them. See *Undaunted Courage* (New York: Simon and Schuster, 1996), p. 187.
7. Bakeless, p. 132.

Into the Unknown

1. DeVoto, p. 92.
2. The men were in the Badlands area, now known as the Missouri Breaks.
3. Cutright, p. 143.
4. Lewis admitted in his journals that he carried his own sack and blanket for the first time in his life—a unique experience for a man who'd grown up served by slaves and who, as an army officer, assigned baggage burdens to soldier aides.
5. DeVoto, p. 133.

The Great Falls

1. DeVoto, p. 138.
2. Betts, p. 28 (Clark quoted).
3. *Ibid.*, p. 26 (Lewis quoted).
4. DeVoto, p. 152.
5. *Ibid.*
6. *Ibid.*, p. 168.
7. Cutright, p. 186.
8. Betts, p. 33 (Lewis quoted).

Finding the Shoshonis

1. Lewis noted that Sacagawea didn't show any emotion. It was his opinion that "if she has enough to eat and a few trinkets to wear . . . she would be perfectly content anywhere"—a remark typical of a time when females were considered flighty and not concerned about important matters. It did not occur to Lewis that Sacagawea was capable of hiding her feelings or smart enough to lead them to her tribe.
2. Ambrose, p. 264 (Lewis quoted).
3. DeVoto, p. 191.
4. Meriwether Lewis, *History of the Expedition Under the Command of Captains Lewis and Clark* (Philadelphia: Bradford and Inskeep; New York: Abm. H. Inskeep, 1814), p. 319.

An Important Meeting

1. "This last account had excited a great degree of curiosity, and they seemed more desirous of seeing this monster than of obtaining the most favorable barter for their horses." Lewis, p. 332. The word *monster* was a curious one for Lewis to use.
2. According to Betts, "York was the principal reason the Shoshonis did not vanish with their horses." See p. 34.
3. Clark noted, "Everything appeared to astonish those people—the appearance of the men, their arms, the canoes, the clothing, my black servant, and the sagacity of Captain Lewis's [pet] dog." http://xroads.virginia.edu /~HYPERJOURNALS/lewis6.html, August 17, 1805.
4. The Shoshonis had once lived and prospered on the Plains, where herds of buffalo made hunting easy. Their enemies, the Blackfeet and the Hidatsas, fighting with guns, forced them to leave the Plains and resettle in the mountains, where game was scarce and they eked out an existence, hungry and poor. They needed buffalo meat for food; the animals' horns for spoons; the hairs for ropes and horse halters; the sinews for sewing leather; and the skins for moccasins, shields, and robes. The Shoshonis did make forays into the Plains to hunt buffalo using bows and arrows, but these excursions often ended in disaster due to enemy attacks.
5. http://xroads.virginia.edu/~HYPER JOURNALS/lewis6.html, August 17, 1805.

Onward!

1. Ronda, p. 154.
2. The reaction of the Flatheads to York is not mentioned in any of the journals of the Lewis and Clark expedition. The information was obtained from stories related by the Flatheads. See Betts, *In Search of York*, p. 36.
3. DeVoto, p. 240.
4. http://xroads.virginia.edu/~HYPER JOURNALS/lewis6.html, September 18, 1805.
5. When Clark mentioned the tribe in his journals, he wrote, "They call themselves *Chop-pun-nish*, or *Pierced Noses*." See Cutright, *Lewis and Clark: Pioneering Naturalists*, p. 214.

6. Betts, p. 58.
7. *Ibid.*, p. 38.

Shooting Rapids

1. http://xroads.virginia.edu/~HYPER JOURNALS/lewis6.html, September 22, 1805.
2. Cutright, p. 221.
3. http://xroads.virginia.edu/~HYPER JOURNALS/lewis6.html, October 24, 1805.
4. The Snake and Columbia Rivers used to produce more salmon than any other place in the world. Fishermen used to catch a ton or more of fish in one day. Salmon runs of this magnitude no longer exist. Catches have diminished as a result of dam construction and pollution.
5. Cutright, p. 232.
6. Ronda, p. 177.

Dampened Spirits

1. DeVoto, p. 295.
2. http://xroads.virginia.edu/~HYPER JOURNALS/lewis7.html, December 30, 1805.
3. *Ibid.*, December 28, 1805.
4. The Chinooks squeezed the foreheads of their babies between two boards so that the front of their heads grew flat in a straight line from the tip of the nose to the top of the head. This shape was beautiful in their eyes, but ugly to whites.
5. Cutright, p. 252.
6. http://xroads.virginia.edu/~HYPER JOURNALS/lewis7.html, March 18, 1806.

3. Homeward Bound

1. "It was at once deemed inexpedient to wait the arrival of the salmon as that would detain us so large a portion of the season that it is probable we would not reach the United States before the ice would close the Missouri." DeVoto, p. 338.
2. An artillery match is specially made for igniting gunpowder.
3. The roots, called *wappatoo*, were described in the journals as a food that is never out of season. See Lewis, *History of the Expedition Under the Command of Captains Lewis and Clark*, vol. 2, p. 224.
4. http://xroads.virginia.edu/~HYPER JOURNALS/lewis7.html, May 5, 1806.
5. DeVoto, p. 369.

York's Mission

1. Ambrose, p. 359.
2. DeVoto, p. 397.
3. *Ibid.*, p. 398.

Return to St. Louis

1. Cutright, p. 302.
2. http://xroads.virginia.edu/~HYPER JOURNALS/lewis8.html, June 16, 1806.
3. Betts, p. 50.
4. http://xroads.virginia.edu/~HYPER JOURNALS/lewis8.html, June 27, 1806.
5. *Ibid.*, p. 31.
6. DeVoto, p. 465.

7. *Ibid.*, p. 474.
8. Newspaper clippings from the Filson Historical Society.

4. Forgotten Man

1. Jackson, p. 364.
2. Holmberg, p. 101. More direct routes across the continent were found later. See also note, p. 109.
3. *Ibid.*, p. 160.
4. *Ibid.*, p. 183.
5. *Ibid.*, p. 201. See also p. 144: "I have been obliged [to] whip almost all my people."
6. Betts, p. 112.

Illustration Credits

The illustrations were selected by Rhoda Blumberg. Cover, title page, 13, 81, courtesy of Ed Hamilton; cover, page 81, Bitterroot Mountains, courtesy of the National Park Service; pages iv–v, 10, maps by Mike Eagle; page 2, *Alic, a Faithful and Humerous Old Servant*, by Benjamin Henry Latrobe, Maryland Historical Society; pages 3, 9, New York Public Library; pages 4, 6, 11, 12, 17, 25, 53, 54, 78, Library of Congress; page 5, Library of Virginia; page 14, Independence National Historical Park; page 17, Missouri Historical Society; page 21, American Philosophical Society; page 23, National Museum of American Art, Smithsonian Institution; page 26, *Pachtüwa-Chtä, Arikara Man*, by Karl Bodmer, Joslyn Art Museum, Omaha, Nebraska, gift of Enron Art Foundation; page 27, *York*, by Charles M. Russell, Montana Historical Society; page 29, *Mandan Village*, by George Catlin, American Museum of Natural History; page 30, *Mandan Buffalo Dance*, by George Catlin, National Museum of American Art, Smithsonian Institution; page 31, American Museum of Natural History; page 32, *Buffalo Chase in Winter, Indians on Snowshoes*, by George Catlin, National Museum of American Art, Smithsonian Institution; page 33, *Mint, a Pretty Girl*, by George Catlin, National Museum of American Art, Smithsonian Institution; page 35, Peabody Museum of Archaeology and Ethnology; page 37, *Citadel Rock on the Upper Missouri*, by Karl Bodmer, Joslyn Art Museum; page 38, *Capt. Lewis at the Black Eagle Falls of the Missouri River—June 13, 1805*, by Olaf C. Seltzer, from the collection of the Gilcrease Museum, Tulsa, Oklahoma; page 40, *Lewis and Clark at the Great Falls of the Missouri, Friday, June 14, 1805*, by Olaf C. Seltzer, from the collection of the Gilcrease Museum; page 42, *Big Bend on the Upper Missouri, 1900 Miles above St. Louis*, by George Catlin, National Museum of American Art, Smithsonian Institution; page 44, Joslyn Art Museum; page 46, *Shoshone Caressing His Horse*, by Alfred Jacob Miller, Stark Museum of Art; page 47, *Máhchis-Níhka, Mandan Man*, by Karl Bodmer, Joslyn Art Museum; page 49, Bitterroot Mountains, photo courtesy of the USDA Forest Service; page 50, Smithsonian Institution National Anthropological Archives; page 55, *Captain William Clark of the Lewis and Clark Expedition Meeting with the Indians of the Northwest*, by Charles M. Russell, Sid Richardson Collection of Western Art; page 57, *The Great Explorers*, by Frederic Remington, Library of Congress; page 59, *Chinook Lodge*, by Paul Kane, Royal Ontario Museum; page 60, Missouri Historical Society; page 61, *Chinook Indian—Columbia River*, by A. J. Millet, Walters Art Gallery; page 65, *A Skin Lodge of an Assiniboin Chief*, by Charles Bodmer, American Museum of Natural History; page 69, Washington State Historical Society; page 70, *Mehkskéhme-Sukáhs, Piegan Blackfeet Chief*, by Karl Bodmer, Joslyn Art Museum; page 71, *Lodge Interior*, by Paul Kane, Stark Museum of Art; page 72, *Interior of a Mandan Earth Lodge*, by Karl Bodmer, Joslyn Art Museum; page 74, Filson Historical Society; page 76, *Rocky Mountain Fort*, by Paul Kane, Royal Ontario Museum.

Bibliography

Ambrose, Stephen. *Undaunted Courage*. New York: Simon and Schuster, 1996.

Appleman, Roy. *Lewis and Clark: Historic Places*. Washington: National Park Service, 1975.

Aptheker, Herbert, ed. *A Documentary History of the Negro People*. Secaucus, N.J.: Citadel Press, 1973.

Bakeless, John. *Lewis and Clark: Partners in Discovery*. New York: William Morrow, 1947.

Betts, Robert B. *In Search of York*. Boulder, Colo.: Colorado Associated University Press, 1985.

Blassingame, John W. *The Slave Community*. New York: Oxford University Press, 1970.

Blumberg, Rhoda. *The Incredible Journey of Lewis and Clark*. New York: Lothrop, Lee and Shepard, 1987.

Cutright, Paul Russell. *Lewis and Clark: Pioneering Naturalists*. Urbana, Ill.: University of Illinois Press, 1969.

Davis, David Brion. *The Problem of Slavery in the Age of Revolution*. Ithaca, N.Y.: Cornell University Press, 1975.

DeVoto, Bernard, ed. *The Journals of Lewis and Clark*. Boston: Houghton Mifflin, 1953.

Elkins, Stanley. *Slavery: A Problem in American Institutional and Intellectual Life*. New York: Grosset and Dunlap, 1963.

Franklin, John Hope. *From Slavery to Freedom: A History of Negro Americans*. New York: Knopf, 1974.

Genovese, Eugene D. *Roll, Jordan, Roll: The World the Slaves Made*. New York: Pantheon Books, 1976.

Hakim, Joy. *History of U.S.* New York: Oxford University Press, 1999.

Harding, Vincent. *There Is a River: The Black Struggle for Freedom in America*. New York: Harcourt Brace Jovanovich, 1981.

Holmberg, James J. *Dear Brother: Letters of William Clark to Jonathan Clark*. New Haven, Conn.: Yale University Press, 2002.

Jackson, Donald. *Letters of the Lewis and Clark Expedition 1783–1854*. Urbana, Ill.: University of Illinois Press, 1962.

Lewis, Meriwether. *History of the Expedition Under the Command of Captains Lewis and Clark*. New York: A. S. Barnes, 1904.

———. *History of the Expedition Under the Command of Captains Lewis and Clark*. 2 vols. Philadelphia: Bradford and Inskeep; New York: Abm. H. Inskeep, 1814.

Lowie, Robert. *Indians of the Plains*. New York: McGraw Hill, 1954.

www.pbs.org/lewisandclark/

Ronda, James P. *Lewis and Clark Among the Indians*. Lincoln, Nebr.: University of Nebraska Press, 1984.

Steffen, Jerome O. *William Clark: Jeffersonian Man on the Frontier*. Norman, Okla.: University of Oklahoma Press, 1977.

Thwaites, Reuben Gold, ed. *Original Journals of the Lewis and Clark Expedition*, 8 vols. New York: Dodd, Mead, 1904–5.

http://xroads.virginia.edu/~HYPER JOURNALS/lewis.html

Index